Understanding and Preventing Suicide

Plenary Papers of the First
Combined Meeting of the AAS and IASP

Edited by
Ronald Maris, Ph.D.

PRINTED IN THE UNITED STATES OF AMERICA

Last digit is print number: 9 8 7 6 5 4 3 2 1
ISBN 0-89862-583-1

Notes on Contributors

Kalle Achté, MD, is Professor and Chairman of the Department of Psychiatry, University of Helsinki, Finland. Dr. Achté is a past president of the International Association for Suicide Prevention. His most recent publications concern cancer as a life crisis, stress and psychosomatics, and a psychodynamic study of psychogeriatrics.

Jewelle Taylor Gibbs, PhD, is Associate Professor of Social Welfare at the University of California at Berkeley. Her research on black youth suicide received the 1987 McCormick Award from the American Association of Suicidology. She is the editor of *Young, Black, and Male in America: An Endangered Species?* (Auburn House, 1988). Dr. Gibbs's research concerns adolescent psychology, specifically the psychosocial problems of minority-group adolescents.

Madelyn S. Gould, PhD, MPH, David Shaffer, MD, and Marjorie Kleinman, MS. Dr. Gould is Assistant Professor of Psychiatry and Public Health (Epidemiology) and Director of Epidemiology in Child Psychiatry at Columbia University, College of Physicians and Surgeons; she is also a research scientist at the New York State Psychiatric Institute. Dr. Shaffer is Irving Phillips Professor of Child Psychiatry at Columbia University and Director of the Department of Child Psychiatry at the New York State Psychiatric Institute. Ms. Kleinman is a biostatistician in the Division of Child Psychiatry at Columbia University.

Norman Kreitman, MD, is Director of the Medical Research Council's Unit for Epidemiological Studies in Psychiatry, Edinburgh, Scotland. He is also Professor of Psychiatry at the University of Edinburgh. His research interests include suicide and parasuicide, alcoholism, and depression. In 1977 he edited *Parasuicide* (Wiley). He received the Dublin Award of the American Association of Suicidology in 1987.

John T. Maltsberger, MD, is Lecturer on Psychiatry at the Harvard Medical School (Massachusetts General Hospital) and is in the private practice of psychiatry in Boston. Dr. Maltsberger has devoted a major portion of his professional career to the psychodynamic study and psychotherapy of patients with suicidal intent. His most recent book is *Suicide Risk: The Formulation of Clinical Judgment* (New York University Press, 1986).

Cynthia R. Pfeffer, MD, is Associate Professor of Clinical Psychiatry at Cornell University Medical College, and Chief of the Child Psychiatry Inpatient Unit at New York Hospital–Westchester Division. She was the president of the American Association of Suicidology in 1986–1987. She is the author of *The Suicidal Child* (Guilford Press, 1986) and has received the Stengel Award from the International Association for Suicide Prevention for her contributions in the field of suicide prevention. She has lectured and published extensively on the subject of childhood and suicidal behavior. In 1981 she received the Young Contributors Award of the American Association of Suicidology.

David P. Phillips, PhD, and Lundie L. Carstensen, MS. Dr. Phillips is Professor of Sociology at the University of California at San Diego. He is author of numerous scientific articles on the media, contagion, suggestibility, and suicide. In 1983, he received the Shneidman Award from the American Association of Suicidology and the sociopsychological prize from the American Association for the Advancement of Science. Most recently, he published two papers in the *New England and Journal of Medicine* (September 11, 1986, and September 24, 1987) concerning the effects of televised movies about suicides on teenage suicide rates and clusters. Dr. Phillips is currently studying suicides and the Vietnam War, occupational suicides, and the distribution of suicides by age. Mr. Carstensen is a PhD graduate student in sociology at the University of California at San Diego.

Leo Rangell, MD, is Clinical Professor of Psychiatry at the University of California at Los Angeles, and Clinical Professor of Psychiatry (Psychoanalysis) at the University of California at San Francisco. He is past president (twice) of the American Psychoanalytic Association, and past president (twice) of the International Psycho-Analytic Association. He was awarded a Guggenheim Fellowship, and was a Fellow at the Center for Advanced Study in the Behavioral Sciences at Stanford. Dr. Rangell is the author of some 300 scientific publications, including the book *The Mind of Watergate: An Exploration of the Compromise of Integrity*.

Erwin Ringel, MD, is Professor of Medical Psychology at the University of Vienna (Austria). He was founder (1960) and first president of the International Association for Suicide Prevention. Professor Ringel has published 262 scientific papers and 13 books dealing with the subjects of suicide prevention, psychosomatic medicine, social psychology, and the theory of neurosis. In 1986 he was awarded the Austrian Medal of Honor for Arts and Sciences.

Edwin S. Shneidman, PhD, is Professor of Thanatology at the University of California at Los Angeles School of Medicine. He was the founder (1968) of the American Association of Suicidology. His most recent books are *Voices of Death* (Harper & Row, 1980) and *Definition of Suicide* (Wiley, 1985). His current research studies focus on personal documents and on the role of septuagenaria within the life course.

UNDERSTANDING AND PREVENTING SUICIDE
Plenary Papers of the First Combined Meeting
of the AAS and IASP

Preface: Overview and Discussion

Ronald Maris, PhD

University of South Carolina Center for the Study of Suicide

This special issue of *Suicide and Life-Threatening Behavior* (Vol. 18, No. 1) is the third in the last 5 years. The first was *Suicide and Ethics* (Vol. 13, No. 4, 1983, with M. P. Battin) and the second was *Biology of Suicide* (Vol. 16, No. 2, Summer 1986). A fourth special issue is now being planned: *Strategies for Studying Suicide*, with Irma Land, MEd, and Eve Móscicki, ScD, MPH, of the National Institute of Mental Health (NIMH). *Understanding and Preventing Suicide* is a collection of most of the plenary papers from the first combined meeting of the American Association of Suicidology (AAS) and the International Association for Suicide Prevention (IASP) in San Francisco (May 1987).

All of the special issues of *Suicide and Life-Threatening Behavior* are designed to focus on a timely and important suicide topic in depth from different theoretical and methodological perspectives. Often the topics chosen are those that I and the Consulting Editors of *Suicide and Life-Threatening Behavior* believe have not gotten enough attention in the past (e.g., the psychobiology of suicide, rational suicide). To examine these special topics, *Suicide and Life-Threatening Behavior* brings in the very best experts available—including specialists who are not necessarily members of AAS, as such special issues serve an expansive, synthesizing function. For better or worse, we also try to keep suicide intervention and control issues clearly in mind.

This special issue is not distinguished so much by the uniqueness of its topic as it is by the distinguished quality of its scholar/authors (see "Notes on Contributors"). The experience and skills of the plenary participants at the historic San Francisco international meeting were striking. To speak selfishly, this volume is an opportunistic *carpe diem*. All 10 chapters substantively address suicide understanding, intervention, and prevention issues and dilemmas, especially from the perspectives of the psychiatric, sociological, and behavioral sciences.

In the pages that follow, readers will witness a lively interplay of diverse professional disciplinary approaches to the study and prevention of suicide. In some papers, theories and hypotheses are salient; in others, methodology is emphasized. In both cases, authors attempt to consider the substantive applications of their theories and methods to suicide and suicide prevention—which, after all, is how it should be in an applied scientific journal.

As editor, it is both my privilege and my responsibility to introduce each chapter and to debate some of its key arguments. I make no claim to be summarizing the chapters or even to be emphasizing their most important points. Each contribution deserves to be read in its entirety. I trust the contributors realize my admiration and respect for all of them. Let me now, in the remaining pages of this preface, turn briefly to each chapter in chronological order.

Chapter 1. At this 20th annual conference, AAS founder Dr. Edwin Shneidman tells us that his dreams for AAS in 1968 have become a reality. He then lists some 18 new developments in suicidology—including (1) a new sense of legitimacy for the study of suicide, (2) life cycle issues, (3) challenges to Durkheim and Freud, and (4) suicide prevention as a complex applied issue—and then reviews changes of the last 40 years. Basically, says Shneidman, the roots of suicide have not changed much. However, suicidology has expanded into a multi-disciplinary enterprise. There are now many more sectors of the suicidological pie than in the past. Shneidman warns us not to reduce the study of suicide to any one discipline or profession (e.g., to resist biologizing suicide).

Dr. Shneidman then reviews his now-celebrated 10 commonalities of suicide and his newer "suicidal cubelet" (which predicts maximum suicide lethality with the maximum joint interaction of pain, perturbation, and negative press). Having been a federal official (at NIMH), Dr. Shneidman concludes by discussing suicide prevention as it relates to public policy. For example, he claims that the more identifiable the suicidal risk, the greater the probability of public response. He tells us that we also need to resist a kind of social Darwinism that conceives of suicides as dispensable, unfit individuals. In the presentation of this chapter at the conference, the taped ghostly voices (viz., those of Drs. Choron, Kubie, Stengel, Dublin, and Menninger) from the past (the 1968 AAS annual meeting) then moved and admonished us all about suicide prevention—as did Dr. Shneidman himself about forgetting his birthday (May 13).

Since Dr. Shneidman's reflections as a founder are hortatory, one is reluctant to debate this charming, witty, and thought-provoking man. Dr. Shneidman's enduring gifts to us all are those of a suicidological Linnaeus or Plato. That is, they are mainly taxonomic and ideal. The questions that remain after Dr. Shneidman has done his best (which is considerable) concern empirical issues of various predictive mixes (interactions) of his concepts (independent variables) in actual basic types of completed and attempted suicides. One must be a little quantitatively suspicious of a man who employs letters, rather than numbers, for his book chapters (in *Definition of Suicide*; Shneidman, 1985)!

I agree with Dr. Shneidman that many important suicidal problems are currently not being studied as a result of public policy and other biases. For example, the Reagan administration has clearly made it very difficult to fund the research of all competent social and behavioral scientists wanting to study suicide. In the recent past, the NIMH has also tended toward biological and epidemiological reductionism even for the limited funds available for suicide research. Of course, one needs to be wary as well of the pitfalls of *any* reductionism, including those of idiographic clinical psychology. No single reductionism is more or less absurd than any other. Having Gerald Brown and Frederick Goodwin draw the spinal fluid of prisoners to test the levels of 5-HIAA (a metabolite of serotonin) in suicide attempters is just as legitimate and fascinating as having Saul Bellow, Isaac Asimov, Carl Sagan, and Karl Menninger read and debate *The Inman Diaries* (Aaron, 1985).

Chapter 2. Professor Erwin Ringel, Dr. Shneidman's European counterpart, gives us his founder's perspective on the history of IASP. He reflects that effective suicide prevention required deviation from important societal norms in Austria (viz., those of the Catholic Church). For example, Professor Ringel found it necessary to resist the suggestion that all suicide prevention required was to make clients good Catholics, since catholicism forbids suicide. The bulk of this chapter is an argument for the necessity of an international suicide prevention association (IASP).

One important task of IASP is to resist the glorification of suicide (e.g., of rational suicide, or what Dr. Phillips and Mr. Carstensen call "the Werther effect" in Chapter 10 of this volume). Would-be suicides deserve protection from themselves. Each individual life (not just some lives in certain circumstances) is important, says Professor Ringel. History reminds us that society has coerced some groups and individuals to die. Consider the Jews in World War II, or the infirm elderly. Another vital task of IASP is to coordinate individual nations' efforts to study and prevent suicide by sharing knowledge and skills.

IASP also needs to determine how suicide prevention can be discussed in the public media without causing additional suicides through suggestion or contagion. Finally, the primary prevention of suicide worldwide requires international cooperation in correcting the much more general social problems of hunger, social injustice, drug abuse, arms races, pollution, and the like. Paradoxically, in spite of these pressing needs for IASP, membership and financial resources are shrinking with the growth of individual national suicide prevention organizations. Professor Ringel invites us to share in the possible resolution of this problem.

The IASP problem is a complex one; however, having lived and worked in Vienna with Professor Ringel (and in West Berlin) and having attended several IASP conferences, I believe that some differences between the AAS (which seems not to have IASP's financial and membership problems) and IASP are obvious. Although no invidious distinctions are intended, much of the vitality of AAS derives from the active involvement of volunteers and paraprofessionals, even at the level of the AAS presidency. In spite of Dr. Sonneck's crisis intervention work in Vienna (and that of others internationally, most notably in Great Britain), the IASP is still largely a professional medical organization. Drug companies advertise at IASP meetings, but very few at AAS conferences. Has a nonphysician ever been president of IASP? The AAS, on the other hand, has the active participation of diverse professional disciplines and volunteers. Witness, too, the AAS certification of suicide telephone crisis services. I remain convinced that one of the factors that hurt early research and training in suicide prevention in the United States was the reluctance of founders to transfer program leadership to others.

A few smaller points of comment on Professor Ringel's chapter are in order. First, to be consistent, Professor Ringel's principle of deviating from societal norms (e.g., those of the Catholic Church) to manage the suicide problem must extend as well to the permitting of some suicides in the Netherlands (see Diekstra, 1986) or to the Hemlock Society's "assisted deaths" (however, see also Richman, in press). Second, if each individual life is important, it follows that each individual *death* is important, too. In some circumstances individuals need to die (as Robert Kastenbaum once said to me, "just as tired people need to sleep")— not necessarily by suicide, though. Just as societies coerce certain groups to die, they also coerce others to live (e.g., in intensive care units or nursing homes). Finally, Professor Ringel is surely correct that suicide is part and parcel of a more general set of social and personal problems. Pollution can be conceived of as a social overdose or nuclear war as mass suicide. Many individuals' suicidal desperation is socially constructed and produced. The cure is to rectify the social injustice, not just the individual pathology. Of course, broad social, economic, and aggressive conditions are more difficult to change.

Chapter 3. The immediate past president of AAS, Dr. Cynthia Pfeffer, makes a strong plea for an interdisciplinary approach to the study of suicide and suicide prevention. She argues that suicide is at once universal or generic (e.g., biologically or developmentally) and specific (e.g., culturally). Like the psychiatrist she is, Dr. Pfeffer considers three individual cases to illustrate her broad argument that we know much about suicidal dynamics already and that a multidisciplinary approach to suicide prevention is the preferred one. For example, the title character in Willa Cather's short story "Paul's Case" exhibits many relatively universal or even contemporary suicidal traits (e.g., depression, social isolation, constricted thinking, etc.), even though his is a fictional case. A second case is the memories of Thomas Berhard when he was a teenager in an Austrian boarding school. Berhard reports social contagion and social pressure effects in the boys' school, inducing many suicidal thoughts and some actual suicides. In a second fictional case, Pfeffer discusses D. H. Lawrence's short story "The Rocking-Horse Winner," which concerns a young child (also named Paul) driven to a premature death by psychosis with an organic component. Dr. Pfeffer reminds us not to forget the past and not to let our professional blinders prevent us from utilizing diverse disciplinary approaches to understanding and controlling suicide (e.g., techniques such as brain imaging).

I find little contest in Dr. Pfeffer's paper. Readers will notice that she is much more favorably disposed toward biological theories and methods than Dr. Shneidman is. We have to ask ourselves why this should be so. Of course, Dr. Pfeffer is a physician and Dr. Shneidman is a clinical psychologist. Although this explanation is much too simple, we should never underestimate what professional training and vested interest can do to distort our perceptions. However, probably both Drs. Pfeffer and Shneidman would resist biological reductionism.

Issue can be taken with Dr. Pfeffer's data. Three individual cases chosen nonrandomly do not a data base make. Typically, physicians study their patients; this clearly introduces an immense source of bias. Patients often ask for help (what about untreated populations?) or are "merely" nonfatal suicide attempters. What this often means is that we have preconceptions about the etiology of suicide *from other sources*, and use a biased sample of individuals (viz., patients) to validate our biases (more generously, our "insights"). Contrast the approaches of Dr. Pfeffer with those of Drs. Gould and Phillips and their colleagues (in Chapters 9 and 10; see below). Of course, properly sampled individual case histories can tell us a great deal about suicides that epidemiology and sociology cannot.

Case histories like those presented by Dr. Pfeffer tell us next to nothing about the complex, detailed empirical interactions of specific independent variables causing self-destructive behaviors or ideations. There is a dangerous complacency in the argument that we already know most of the important factors in suicide and how they operate. Consider depressive illness or alcoholism. The actual empirical associations of just these two traditional presuicidal variables with specific suicide types are enormously complex. In some cases and circumstances, both depressive illness and alcoholism actually *protect* us from completed suicide. In others, depression and alcoholism have no relationship to suicide at all. Thus, it is cavalier to say that we already know a lot about the etiology of suicide without qualification or caveat. One could just as easily argue that we truly understand very little about specific suicidal dynamics yet.

Chapter 4.   Eminent psychoanalyst Leo Rangell concentrates upon the immediate psychoanalytic surround of the decision to commit suicide. His largely theoretical chapter is written from the perspective of psychoanalytic decision theory. This is not to argue that there is not indecision or compromise in the decision to suicide. Dr. Rangell claims there is. In fact, not everything that follows from a decision was intended by it (says Dr. Rangell); suicide can be partly an accident.

Dr. Rangell contends that the range of motivations for suicide is not all that wide. For example, suicide is often external aggression turned against oneself. This may happen when loss of love allows aggression to dominate one's libido. Suicide can also result from a chronic or acute lowering of self-regard. In such circumstances, the would-be suicide often feels devoid of any future (i.e., is hopeless). Suicide can result as well from manic excitement, immortality wishes, or attempted mastery over traumatic helplessness.

We are reminded that suicide is a symptom, not a diagnosis, and that while the state of being suicidal can be analyzed, the act of suicide cannot be. Suicidal thoughts, like all human thoughts, are experimental actions. Suicidal thoughts and death instincts are opposed by life instincts. Sometimes, when unconscious wishes to die gain the upper hand, they are fueled by attachment behavior or contagion (such as in teenage suicide clusters). In other cases, sudden shame can provoke an acute suicidal crisis. In still others, suicides fear survival more than dying. Suicide can even be an attempt to master fear of death or castration fears by paradoxically choosing death.

Dr. Rangell has written a long and profound chapter. It is difficult to respond to it in a few perfunctory remarks. However, some aspects of his chapter jump out at the reader. For example, note the types of variables in Dr. Rangell's suicide "equations." Suicide is held to result variously from loss of love, castration fear, sudden and powerful shame, low self-regard, hopelessness, death instincts, and so on. How different from the independent variables of the epidemiologist's or sociologist's etiological factors in suicide! If we are all studying the same behaviors, why do some of us see the primary causes so differently? And who is right? Why is it so difficult to combine the major variables of several different disciplines and empirically test their relative importance with adequate samples of suicides and controls? Note, too, that Dr. Rangell's concepts, ideas, and arguments are highly abstract, even compared to Dr. Maltsberger's concepts in the following chapter.

As one might expect from a psychoanalyst, Dr. Rangell argues for many nonrational components in the dynamics of suicide. I would like to call attention to the salience of the loss of love. Although we need to be as professional and expert as possible in suicide prevention, often what the would-be suicide needs desperately and is unable to give or receive is not professional expertise, but rather is love; for example, he or she may be devoid of what Dr. Avery Weisman calls a "significant utter." Furthermore, if there are many nonrational, affective, or instinctive forces determining the suicidal act, then is it really a *decision* to die at all? One could argue that many suicides are psychologically or culturally obligatory or compulsory, such as the suicides of Japanese military officers after the loss of World War II, or suicides as a result of psychosis, stress, perturbation, or the like. It is also not clear in Rangell's argument whether the rationality in the decision to suicide is that of the suicide himself or herself or that of the psychoanalytic observer.

A final comment: Many suicidal actions are paradoxical. For example, Dr. Rangell claims that some suicides are motivated by the "fear of survival." I would like to generalize Dr. Rangell's point. That is, many acts of self-destruction are paradoxically intended to be self-preservative, and in the short run may in fact be self-preservative. Elsewhere, I have argued (Maris, 1971) that sexual promiscuity or alcoholism are usually adaptive in the short run. Although they are not the preferred defenses, many such coping attempts are all that are keeping people alive until more appropriate responses become viable. It is important to realize that such people have limited adaptive repertoires and that partially self-destructive coping mechanisms are in large part intended to be survival efforts, not suicidal acts.

Chapter 5.   In this chapter and in a recent book (1986), psychiatrist John T. Maltsberger warns us that the traditional mental status examination and clinical intuition or empathetic judgment are not sufficient to predict suicide. The formulation of clinical judgment about suicide risk requires a much more disciplined method. According to Dr. Maltsberger, assessing suicidal risk involves the following five components:

1. The patient's past response to stress.
2. Vulnerability to life-threatening affects.
3. Exterior sustaining resources.
4. Death fantasies.
5. Capacity for reality testing.

Dr. Maltsberger then discusses and elaborates these five components:
    1. The patient's past response to stress includes lifelong coping patterns. Suicidal patients often have vulnerability to despair.

2. Life-threatening affects include (a) aloneness (which is feeling beyond hope), (b) self-contempt (self-contempt "burns"; there is no merit in the self), and (c) murderous rage (rage is more than simple anger).

3. Other people, one's work, and special aspects of self (such as pride in one's body or physical capabilities) are the main exterior sustaining resources. Dr. Maltsberger cautions that resources may be there, but are refused or otherwise unavailable for various reasons.

4. One particularly suicidogenic death fantasy is that death is not total cessation, but is egression (often to a better condition or place).

5. The suicide-prone individual may not know that others love him or her, that there is hope, that his or her work is good, and so on.

Again, in this terse and highly focused practical chapter, we are offered ideal types. Note that Dr. Maltsberger's ideal types are less abstract than those of Drs. Rangell or Shneidman. One wonders where these five components of clinical judgment have come from. For example, are they derived solely from the biased sample of a few suicidal patients Dr. Maltsberger has had in his practice over the years? It is also curious that there are five components and not (say) three or twelve. It would be useful as well to know how we could objectively measure concepts or variables such as aloneness or murderous rage, in order that they would not be confused with mere lonesomeness or simple anger.

Stress effects tend to sum physiologically. This means that stress responses late in life are different from those early in life. For example, if we have a finite number of adaptations to stress, then we do not necessarily get used to it or get better able to handle it. Resources like work also change (in their worth) over time. Although we may be incredibly successful in our work, at some point in our lives work may not nurture or support us as well as before or as well as people do.

Finally, one should not overlook concepts like "pronoia" (the delusion that people like or love us). Reality testing can be at fault in a number of different directions. That is, not only are we not aware of how much people love us or how good our work is, but also we often perceive *more* interest in us or positive evaluation of our work than actually exists (i.e., are "pronoid," not paranoid).

Chapter 6. With all the recent emphasis on suicide among youthful populations, Dr. Kalle Achté, past president of IASP, reminds us that suicide rates are highest among the elderly. In one Finnish study of subjects under 25 years of age, 34% had a genuine wish to die, but of those over 64 years of age, 76% wished to die. Dr. Achté tells us that a completed suicide is likely to be a middle-aged or older male, from a large birth cohort, in deteriorating health, who becomes depressed and then shoots himself (or at least has many of these traits).

Dr. Achté claims that elderly suicides are more likely than younger suicides to be multifactorial; for example, the older individuals are more likely to be lonely, isolated, and depressed, and to have somatic illnesses. Numerous losses also characterize older suicides. The resultant loneliness often leads to depressive illness among the elderly. Injuries to self-esteem are common in old age as well, particularly feelings of emptiness and uselessness. Moreover, the elderly external appearance commonly no longer corresponds well with internal body image. Depressive disorders in the elderly often present as somatic symptoms.

Aggressive impulses previously neutralized by work and social life earlier in life now break through more easily. Dr. Achté claims that the problems of the elderly are partly social, in the sense that society offers little of worth for the elderly to do. Psychoanalytically, elderly suicide is therefore usually not a wish to die, but rather an attempt to free oneself from the inner conflicts Dr. Achté describes.

I agree with Dr. Achté that focus on youth suicide can cause neglect of more fundamental paradigmatic suicidal types. Suicidologists need to study the entire range of the life cycle, including middle-aged as well as elderly suicides. However, I am not convinced that elderly suicides are more likely to be multifactorial than are younger suicides. Of course, it is probably true that the longer one lives, the more likely it is that numerous life problems will develop. Most suicide tolerance thresholds are gradually breached by accumulated stresses and developmental strains (I refer to this phenomenon generally as "suicidal careers"; see Maris, 1981) and youthful suicides often result from relatively few factors' acutely overwhelming the young person. For example, Phillips and Carstensen report (see Chapter 10) that the contagion or modeling effect is much more powerful in teenagers than in adults (viz., a rise in teen suicide rates of about 22% vs. 4–12% in other age groups 3–7 days after a publicized suicide). However, I suspect that if one looks closely at youthful suicides, they are just as multifactorial as elderly suicides; it is just that the factors in the two age groups are different.

Dr. Achté also reminds us to tease out interaction effects in suicidal dynamics (e.g., those involving depression, aggression, and work). We have seen that elderly losses can lead to depression, or that aggressive impulses may be fairly constant over the life cycle while outlets for aggression can change. To illustrate, work patterns, sexual activities, or available friends may cease to be as viable outlets as they were earlier in the life cycle.

Finally, Dr. Achté argues that it is more important to conceptualize suicide as freeing oneself of inner conflicts, not simply as an uncomplicated wish to die. Presumably, if inner conflicts can be resolved, then suicide should be less necessary. For example, if we can cope with aging or minimize ageism, the elderly suicide rate should be reduced. Religion can be especially helpful in the resolution of conflict in the aged. Still, the real question is whether most inner conflicts of the elderly can in fact be resolved short of death or suicide (Maris, 1982). How avoidable in individual suicide cases among the aged are loss, depression, negative body image, and so forth? Is a malevolent or punitive society or the natural order (e.g., biological imperatives) causing suicidal crises for the aged?

Chapter 7. Dr. Norman Kreitman, winner of the Louis I. Dublin Award in 1987 for his work on parasuicide, tells us that basically there have been two traditions in suicide research: the psychiatric and the sociological. The early debate between the Frenchmen Esquirol and Durkheim concerned primarily whether or not mental illness can explain suicide rates (Durkheim argued that it cannot). Today, most modern sociologists and psychiatrists agree that mental illness is clearly a major factor in suicide.

One of the central methodological issues in suicide research has been whether suicide "facts" (e.g., as in the vital statistics) are subjectively constructed by medical examiners or others (i.e., are not facts at all), or whether they are relatively valid and reliable data. Dr. Kreitman replies that we can question the meanings of suicide and still have an empirical science of suicide. A bigger problem is that there has been relatively little interaction between sociologists and psychiatrists and their two traditions in the study of suicide. Dr. Kreitman concludes that an integration of the two traditions is needed.

Of course, contrary to Dr. Kreitman's claim, there are more than two traditions in suicide research. Obviously, there have also been at least major biological, economic, public health, epidemiological, psychological, anthropological, and historical traditions in the study of suicide (Maris, 1986). Even within psychiatry and sociology, there are more than two traditions. One immediately thinks of ethnomethodologists (e.g., Jack Douglas) versus Durkheimian sociologists (David Phillips), or psychobiologists (Herman van Praag) versus "cognitive" psychiatric researchers (Aaron Beck).

Recent careful empirical studies (e.g., Pescosolido & Mendelsohn, 1986) suggest that although systematic misrepresenting of suicides exists, it has little impact on variables used to test sociological theories of suicide. Also, the alternatives proposed to using vital statistics or survey data of third-party respondents to study suicide (e.g., Douglas, 1967) have their own major methodological problems. For one, social constructionists tend to study first-person accounts of nonfatal attempted suicides, not completed suicides at all. Furthermore, social constructionists have not been able to generate large, reliable random samples that allow the scientific study of suicide. Constructionists have been much better at criticism. However, in defense of social constructionists, it is worrisome that those social scientists in the Durkheimian tradition employing vital statistics to study suicide have arrived at such different results using supposedly accurate data and objective procedures.

Dr. Kreitman is aware that the integration of diverse traditions in the study of suicide is in fact well under way and has been for years. This very journal (*Suicide and Life-Threatening Behavior*) has promoted and published interdisciplinary research between psychiatrists and sociologists for almost 20 years now. I myself have a PhD in sociology and was Associate Professor of Psychiatry at the Johns Hopkins Medical School. In Dr. Kreitman's own psychiatry department in Edinburgh, Dr. Stephen Platt is a medical sociologist working in psychiatry. There are also many other sociologists working in psychiatry (e.g., Dr. Carol Huffine from Berkeley, California).

Of course, Dr. Kreitman is right that there are considerable obstacles to the interdisciplinary study of suicide. Professionals tend to have career tracks within their own disciplines. Our degrees and disciplines (e.g., as a physician/psychiatrist or a sociologist) dictate the journals we need to publish in (e.g., to get tenure or raises), the research grant monies we will be able to get, the consulting opportunities we are asked to participate in, and so on. The truly interdisciplinary suicide synthesizers have often been regarded as disciplinary turncoats. For example, psychiatrists or sociologists working primarily on suicide research often find themselves regarded as marginal to their own departments. Thus, unfortunately, interdisciplinary research on suicide frequently *is* professional suicide itself.

Chapter 8. Dr. Jewelle Taylor Gibbs, Associate Professor of Social Welfare at the University of California (Berkeley) and 1987 winner of the McCormick Award for her study of minority-group suicides, informs us that black suicide, homicide, violence, and accidents are especially likely among the young. Up to now, there has been limited research published on black suicides. We do know that, as with whites, the adolescent suicide rate increase was mainly among older young adult (aged 20–24) males. The adolescent black suicide rate leveled off in 1978 (white adolescent suicide rates leveled off in 1977). However, black suicide and violence are still pressing problems, especially given the young age of the black population (the median age of American blacks recently has been about 26).

Dr. Gibbs has four main goals in her chapter: (1) to assess the reliability and validity of data on youthful black suicide; (2) to evaluate three conceptual perspectives; (3) to specify sociocultural factor differences between black male and female suicides; and (4) to propose strategies for early intervention in youthful black suicides. A few words on each of these four objectives are in order.

1. Some black homicides, accidents, and drug deaths are probably in fact disguised suicides. For this and other reasons, black suicides are underreported.

2. Dr. Gibbs examines the sociological, psychological, and ecological perspectives. She claims that most sociologists fail to account for differences in black male and female suicide rates. Psychologically, the Freudian concept of suicide as object loss and subsequent depressive illness is not very appropriate for young black suicides. More often, young blacks feel rage that gets turned back upon themselves. Ecologically and demographically, Dr. Gibbs calls our attention to the effect of large cohort size encouraging black suicides.

3. Many sociocultural factors are protective against black suicide (e.g., strong and large families, regular church attendance, social organizational participation, community schools, and extended social support networks). Unfortunately, many of these black protective factors have weakened recently.

4. Dr. Gibbs suggests that strategies for early detection of black suicides include (a) clinics and suicide prevention centers located in inner cities; (b) better referrals for black youths known to be at high suicide risk; (c) alleviation of community tensions between the police and black youths; (d) provision of more positive adult black male role models in fatherless homes; (e) better control of lethal weapons; and (f) (as always) funding more research for investigating and preventing minority-group suicide.

In the same way that Dr. Gibbs wisely expands black suicides to include black homicides, accidents, and drug deaths, we need to pay attention to the self-destructive behaviors and suicidal social forces of other, nonblack minority-group members as well. What is to become of social minorities unfortunate enough not to have eloquent advocates like Dr. Gibbs? I refer here to children in general, homosexuals, prisoners, American Indians, Hispanic Americans, and the like.

Attention also needs to be called to minority-group drug deaths. Cynically, one could argue that heroin (or PCP, "crack," etc.) abuse is often tacitly ignored by the white majority, since the primary victims are young members of minority groups. In the same way that young women are chemically imprisoned by their (encouraged) Valium, Librium, and alcohol abuse in their suburban homes, perhaps white middle-class males socially control (and indirectly kill) minorities by allowing inner-city drug abuse? Similarly, black violence (including "victim-precipitated homicide") is most often against other blacks, so why not tacitly permit it (if one is in the white majority)?

Finally, Dr. Gibbs is correct that suicide prevention among young blacks requires primary prevention, in which the economic, educational, and vocational circumstances of young blacks are improved. This requires sweeping changes in social and racial inequalities. For example, in spite of gains in average black income, blacks still earn only about 60% of the average white income (often even with comparable education). Young blacks typically have the highest unemployment rates of any other social group. In short, prevention of suicide among young blacks is not primarily a matter of individual psychiatric or crisis treatment, but rather is one of rectifying broad social and economic injustices for all minorities.

Chapter 9. In a prior paper (Gould & Shaffer, 1986), Drs. Gould and Shaffer suggested an increase in teenage suicides in the New York City area following the broadcast of four fictional television films on suicide (shown in 1984 and 1985). The study reported in this current chapter replicates the previous project in Cleveland–Akron, Dallas–Fort Worth, and Los Angeles–Anaheim–Riverside. Dr. Gould, Dr. Shaffer, and Ms. Kleinman studied only completed suicides 19 years old or younger.

They found that the impact of the televised suicide movies was not uniform across all metropolitan areas. For example, there were (statistically significant) increases in completed suicide after the movies in New York and Cleveland, but not in Los Angeles or Dallas. Gould et al. ruled out experimental weeks in alternate years and acceleration as alternative hypotheses.

In their discussion section, they ask how one could explain geographic differences in suicide response. There could be a "dose effect" (i.e., the more exposure, the more effect). Or there could just be low statistical power to detect an effect (even if it were in fact there). Finally, there might be case completeness variation and aggregate data confusions. Given the time sequence of variables, the consistency of association upon replication, the strength of the associations, and an explanation that is congruent with previous research, Dr. Gould and her coauthors conclude (conditionally, of course, pending further research) that there *is* an imitative effect following media coverage of suicide among teenagers.

The strength of Gould et al.'s research is also its main weakness. It is essentially a very careful, focused, methodological overkill on just one variable (i.e., imitation). For example, this chapter in effect asks, "Does imitation (contagion, media, suggestion, or modeling) cause teen suicide?" Remember Dr. Shneidman's admonition (in Chapter 1) that suicide is a *multi*dimensional malaise. One natural reaction to Gould et al.'s chapter is "What *other* independent variables contribute to teen suicide?" Another question is "What percentage of the teen suicide rate variance is explained by imitation?" Practically, Gould et al. raise far more questions than they answer. We should remember, though, that imitation is not just any old independent variable.

A related query to Dr. Gould and her colleagues is this: "If contagion effects teen suicide, then could they specify the model better?" Others have claimed that if the suicide on television and the would-be real-life suicide are similar (e.g., in age, sex, race, social class, parental situation, etc.), then the imitative effect is greater. One also wonders about receptivity or "priming." That is, are viewers on the edge of the suicidal decision more vulnerable to the suicide film than are those who are not predisposed to suicide anyway? There are many such additional independent variables that need to be incorporated into the imitation causal model and then empirically tested. Of course, such practical extensions are usually not done or are very limited, mainly because the data are not easily available. Much of the epidemiology of suicide is a study of convenience, rather than what actually needs to be done.

Both the Gould et al. chapter and the Phillips and Carstensen chapter that follows raise critical ethical issues concerning freedom of the press, the public's right to know, the probability of causing additional teen suicides, and so on. Paradoxically, it now appears that educational films about suicide prevention actually cause some additional suicides and that this contagion effect is not small (Phillips and Carstensen found about a 22% rise in suicide rates 3–7 days after a suicide story was shown). Short of not showing teen suicide films at all, some commentators have suggested minimizing the effect of the TV media presentation. This could be done by giving the film an "R" or "PG" rating, showing the film only at night, showing it less often or not at times teenagers would be likely to watch television, and so on. Others have suggested viewing the films with a caveat listing its dangers, an advertisement for the local suicide prevention center or community mental health center, a clinical commentary, or even pictures of actual teen suicides to deromanticize teen suicide. Most experts agree that aversion conditioning does not work very well, especially if the viewer is a depressed malignant masochist who wants to punish himself or herself.

Chapter 10. Dr. Phillips and Mr. Carstensen remind us that French sociologist Emile Durkheim argued that imitation does not affect the social suicide rate. From 1897 until about 1974, almost no one contested Durkheim's claim. However, from 1974 until the present, Dr. Phillips has maintained that imitation does not just "precipitate" suicides that would have occurred anyway. In this concluding chapter, Phillips and Carstensen analyze the effects of suicide stories in TV news programs (from 1968 to 1985) on the suicide rates of various social groups.

For males 0–7 days after the stories were broadcast, there were about three more suicides per story; for females, there were about 1.6 more suicides per story—for a total of 4.6 additional suicides per story. Thus, nationwide, 43 televised stories probably produced about 199 extra suicides in California and roughly 2,000 in the United States as a whole. Given 30,000 suicides annually in the United States, this is about a 7% increase.

Phillips and Carstensen find that contagion or the "Werther effect" (after Goethe's character in *The Sorrows of Young Werther*) is quite large for teenagers. For this age group, there was an increase in suicides above the expected rate by 22%. Still, the Werther effect is not as large as the effect of other standard demographic variables (e.g., age, race, sex, and day of the week). So, then, why study contagion? One good reason, say the authors, is that the Werther effect is changeable, but age, race, sex or "blue Mondays" (a day when suicide rates are high) are not.

For example, multiprogram suicide stories produce greater Werther effects. Thus, we could minimize contagion of suicide through running single-program suicide stories, single advertisements, more obscure ads, and/or more neutral commentaries; mentioning negative aspects of suicide (e.g., as we already do in cigarette advertisements); or suggesting alternatives to suicide. Thus, one could change suicide stories in television and other media without omitting them from the news.

Of course, one serious problem with almost all research on modeling or imitation is that the research is unable to determine whether the eventual suicides actually saw or read the media suicide stories. All we really know is that the suicide rate goes up more than expected after publicized suicide stories. A venerable maxim in social science is that association is not causation. It *could* be that suicides subsequent to publicized suicide stories are reacting to some other (third) variable, not to contagion at all. Dr. Phillips has tried very hard over the years to rule these alternative explanations out, but he has never studied actual suicides to see whether they watched the media events (or contrasted those suicides who did watch the suicide media stories with those people who also watched but did not commit suicide).

In a sense, Dr. Phillips's very careful and successful imitation research reminds me of Paul Simon's song, "One Trick Pony." Dr. Phillips has done basically the same procedure now for about 15–20 years. Although he has been quite productive in his methodological doggedness, the creativity is questionable. When I asked him this question recently, he told me a story about three men working with bricks. When asked what they were doing, the first man said that he was making bricks;

the second man said that he was making a wall; and the third man said that he was making a cathedral. I took Dr. Phillips to mean that *he* was making sociological bricks, and that maybe someday, with an accumulated, solid empirical foundation, we can worry about cathedrals. Personally, I don't think cathedrals are usually made that way.

I also wonder why Dr. Phillips has concentrated on contagion and suicide to the virtual exclusion of all other independent variables, other than that it is easier and more practical to do so. Surely, we need more specific comparisons of the effects of variables. For example, how much variance does modeling explain in an explicit regression model with suicide as its dependent variable? What is the relative effect of other independent variables in that same regression model? What are the various interaction effects of modeling and other independent variables? These are basic questions we all need answers to, especially if in most populations imitation increases suicide rates by only 4–12% for only 3–7 days after the publicized suicide stories. Of course, this research would require collecting large amounts of costly data on adequate samples of suicides and controls, which is no small undertaking.

These chapters, then, are most of the plenary papers from the first combined meeting of AAS and IASP. For various reasons, some plenary papers are not included in this special issue. I refer to a session on youth suicide prevention, another on AIDS and rational suicide, and the responses of the Stengel awardees to Dr. Shneidman's and Professor Ringel's presentations. Certainly this volume would have been better if these had been included. I chose to omit them in part because they are more free-standing topics that have and will continue to get a great deal of deserved public attention. Furthermore, they did not fit as well into the theme of this present issue. I hope that readers enjoy the stimulating work that is included here. I thank the contributors for their efforts, and hope that all this will have some impact in our common objective to reduce human suffering, especially premature and unnecessary death.

References

Aaron, D. (Ed.). *The Inman diaries: A public and private confession* (Vols. 1 and 2). Cambridge, Mass.: Harvard University Press, 1985.

Diekstra, R. F. W. The significance of Nico Speijer's suicide: How and when should suicide be prevented? *Suicide and Life-Threatening Behavior*, 1986, *16*, 13–15.

Douglas, J. *The social meanings of suicide*. Princeton, N.J.: Princeton University Press, 1967.

Gould, M. S., & Shaffer, D. The impact of suicide in television movies: Evidence of imitation. *New England Journal of Medicine*, 1986, *315*, 690–694.

Maltsberger, J. T. *Suicide risk: The formulation of clinical judgment.* New York: New York University Press, 1986.

Maris, R. W. Deviance as therapy: The paradox of the self-destructive female. *Journal of Health and Social Behavior,* 1971, *12,* 114–124.

Maris, R. W. *Pathways to suicide.* Baltimore: Johns Hopkins University press, 1981.

Maris, R. W. Rational suicide. *Suicide and Life-Threatening Behavior,* 1982, *12,* 3–16.

Maris, R. W. Preface. In R. W. Maris (Ed.), *The biology of suicide.* New York: Guilford Press, 1986.

Pescosolido, B. A., & Mendelsohn, R. Social causation or social construction of suicide? An investigation into the social organization of official rates. *American Sociological Review,* 1986, *51,* 80–100.

Richman, R. The case against rational suicide [Letter to the editor]. *Suicide and Life-Threatening Behavior,* in press.

Shneidman, E. S. *Definition of suicide.* New York: Wiley, 1985.

CHAPTER 1

Some Reflections of a Founder

Edwin S. Shneidman, PhD

University of California at Los Angeles School of Medicine

When I was in Vienna for the International Association for Suicide Prevention (IASP) meeting in 1985, I saw a stunning exhibition of the art, music, architecture, politics, and psychology of Vienna from 1870 to 1930 at the Kunsterhaus. The exhibition was called *Traum und Wirklichkeit*—"Dream and Reality." For me, the joint meeting of the American Association of Suicidology (AAS) and the IASP in San Francisco could be summed up with this brief sentence: *Ein Traum ist Wirklichkeit geworden*—"A dream has become reality." I was heartened to note the presence of many members from abroad (27 different countries) and from 36 separate states of the United States.

The Founding of the AAS

From 1966 to 1969, between my previous stay at the Los Angeles Suicide Prevention Center and my subsequent stints at Harvard and UCLA, I was at the National Institute of Mental Health (NIMH), serving as the first Chief of the Center for Studies of Suicide Prevention. In 1966 there were three suicide prevention centers in this country; by 1970 there were over 200. Dozens of research projects around the country were supported by the NIMH Center. The *Bulletin of Suicidology*, which later metamorphosed into *Suicide and Life-Threatening Behavior*, was begun. It was a lively period of considerable activity. It became evident to me that the time had come for a national organization relating the study of suicide and suicide prevention. I was determined to try to begin with a special meeting of the best available suicidologists in the country (and one from England). With the help of an old friend, Professor William E. Henry at the University of Chicago, a meeting was scheduled in Chicago on March 20, 1968. I believe that there was as much suicidological talent and experience at that table that day at the Conrad

Hilton Hotel as has even been assembled in one place. The group consisted of Jacques Choron, Louis I. Dublin, Paul Friedman, Robert Havighurst, Lawrence Kubie, Karl Menninger, and Erwin Stengel. They were all then in their 70s and 80s; only Dr. Menninger and Professor Havighurst, bless them, are alive today.

That meeting was a kind of "reconvening" of the famous meeting in Freud's apartment in Vienna in 1910—the meeting of Freud, Adler, Jung, Stekel, and Oppenheim. The 1910 meeting is reported to us in English in Paul Friedman's 1967 edited book *On Suicide*, which was my point of departure. In my comments at the 1968 meeting, I noted that the 1910 meeting was unusual in a number of ways. It was the only meeting held by the Vienna psychoanalytic group on the topic of suicide; the meeting was chaired not by Freud but by Adler; it was held on the temporal threshold (within 1 year) of the splintering of that group; it was the occasion of the first enunciation by Wilhelm Stekel of the psychodynamic formulation that the yearning of the death of the self is the mirrored wish for the death of another; it seemed to stimulate Freud's own thoughts on death and suicide; and it focused on the adolescent and on the role of education in suicide prevention. In all, this was a remarkable set of overt and latent threads.

In addition, in the report of the 1968 meeting, I addressed the issue of what was then new in suicidology. In this effort, I listed and discussed some 18 items, which I am emboldened to summarize here:

1. A new permissiveness to discuss and study suicide and death.
2. A focus on suicide prevention, including its elaborations, especially postvention.
3. Changes in concepts of death, especially (since Menninger) "partial death" and my concept of "subintentioned death."
4. Changes in the format and uses of the death certificate—a forerunner of the concept of the psychological autopsy.
5. An increased understanding of the varieties of intention in self-destruction.
6. A recognition of the pivotal place of ambivalence in suicide.
7. An appreciation of the key role of the significant other in suicide and of the usually dyadic nature of suicide.
8. The role of affective states other than hostility in suicide, especially hopelessness and malignant pessimism.
9. A growing appreciation of the role of age in the human life cycle as it touches suicide.
10. The usefulness of explicating suicidality along the dimensions of perturbation and lethality.

11. An emphasis on the delineation and dissemination of the prodromal clues to suicide—a pivot in the whole prevention movement.
12. The implications of advances in medical techniques related to suicide.
13. The impact of the massive secularization of death and the enormous spiritual and psychological problems created by it.
14. Some new looks at old masters, especially Freud and Durkheim, and the possibility and the obvious challenge to come to this topic through some new portals.
15. Significant changes in the public practice of suicide prevention, especially in the services that ought to be provided.
16. Changes in the patterns of financial and community support for suicide prevention activities.
17. A growing emphasis on assessment, especially of the effectiveness of interventional efforts.
18. The recent appearance of suicide professionalism and the possible role of a new profession, suicidology.

The AAS was founded at the meeting in Chicago. I was blessed with the special help of Avery Weisman, whose counsel was indispensable to me. Of course, I conferred with my mentor Henry Murray. At my request, Calvin Frederick, who was then with me at NIMH, prepared a constitution and a set of by-laws patterned more or less after those of the multidisciplinary American Orthopsychiatric Association. By the end of that day, our dream of an AAS, in our minds at least, was a reality. One year later at our second meeting in New York City, I found myself president. Happily, the organization soon had a life of its own. If the association were to have a motto, it would be "Research, Training, Service."

I now have the pleasure of listing the subsequent presidents of the AAS since 1969: Seymour Perlin, Avery Weisman, Norman Farberow, Jerome Motto, Robert Kastenbaum, Richard McGee, Nancy Allen, Robert Litman, Betsy Comstock, Bruce Danto, Calvin Frederick, Ronald Maris, James Selkin, Gwendolyn Harvey, Joseph Thigpen, Allan Berman, Pamela Cantor, Cynthia Pfeffer, Elizabeth Jones, and President-Elect Charlotte Sanborn—a Who's Who of American suicidology (including, I am pleased to note, a second generation of the younger professionals and workers in our field). What is evident is that the AAS has moved from being an organization of only psychologists and psychiatrists to being truly multidisciplinary. It includes nurses, social workers, sociologists, and health educators; even more, it reflects the role of volunteers and of help-lines, and the issues of accreditation and of standards.

The list of presidents is varied, vibrant, and multitalented, and provides a good augury for our multidisciplinary future.

The topic for the IASP–AAS joint meeting was "Then and Now." What have I seen over the past 40 years in American suicidology? My reflections divide themselves into two categories: those about the phenomena of suicide itself, and those about the practice of suicide prevention within the larger social setting.

The Phenomena of Suicide

In relation to suicidal phenomena (the events themselves), I have seen no great change, nor would I expect to see one in so relatively short a time. By definition, the ubiquities are still there. The basic roots of anguish, psychological pain, thwarted emotions—hate, love, shame, guilt (who has said them better than Shakespeare almost half a millenium ago and Melville a century ago?)—have not changed. Of course, the phenotypic details vary, but the unity themes sound the same old chords. As a small example: Two years ago, with permission, I personally collected all the suicide notes for Los Angeles County for the calendar year 1984. They read pretty much the same as the suicide notes that Norman Farberow and I collected from that same office almost 40 years before. I do believe that the meaning of death and suicide *do* change, as Aries (1975/1981) has so persuasively shown us in *The Hour of Our Death* (a book that covers the past millenium), but the interval between 1968 and 1988, even with everything that has happened in the world, is merely a blip on the screen of these timeless topics. The ubiquities remain.

But the *study* of suicide is another matter. We have seen an expansion of what I consciously tried to promote in my brief tenure at NIMH— an advertent and tenacious multidisciplinarity. I assure you that I do not take credit for this expansion; I simply note its presence and call it to our attention. Today, there are *many* legitimate approaches to the study of suicide, among which can be listed the following:

1. The literary and personal-documents approach, including the use of suicide notes and suicide diaries. I am currently especially interested in the potentialities for concerted, cooperative studies of the recently published *Inman Diary* (Aaron, 1985), and, along these lines, who has told us more about the inside of suicide than Dostoyevsky, Tolstoy, Flaubert, Melville, and Kate Chopin?

2. Theological and philosophical approaches, where our late friend Jacques Choron was so effective.

3. The demographic approach—an indispensable background for further work—where one thinks of John Graunt, Johann Sussmilch, and Louis I. Dublin.

4. The sociocultural approach—for example, between Japan and the United States (in this connection, see Iga's [1986] *The Thorn in the Chrysanthemum*.

5. The sociological approach, with several members of the AAS at its intellectual forefront.

6. The dyadic, interpersonal, familial approaches—our recent leaders have had much to say here.

7. The psychodynamic approach, exemplified by Freud, Menninger, and several of our past presidents.

8. The psychological approach, emphasizing psychological pain, constriction, and thwarted needs, as explicated by Henry Murray.

9. The psychiatric approach—the mental illness and disease approach, focusing on depression.

10. The constitutional and genetic approach, involving both cohort and DNA studies.

11. Biological and biochemical approaches, with currently ambiguous but potentially thrilling potentialities.

12–15. Legal, ethical approaches; the preventional approach; systems theory approaches; and political, global, and supernational approaches. I have eschewed naming notable AAS members in connection with these only because I fear to omit many who should be included.

But one can clearly see that the study of suicide is a never-completed circle, containing many legitimate sectors or fields or approaches. The only illegitimate approach to this multidisciplinary pie is for someone to plant a fork in one spot and pronounce that *that* sector, *that* way of looking at things, is the whole pie. But this point is too obvious to belabor. The blessing of our lives is that we have come upon this field that was nascent, dormant, and quiescent, and in our own lifetimes have awakened it so that it has become a legitimate area for concern and for scholarly study. Nowadays, one can say "I am a suicidologist" and hold one's head high.

Speaking of the various sectors of the suicidal pie, in my own recent publications I have aimed, in some small way, to clarify the *psychological* sector of this fascinating etiological circle. In pursuit of this intellectual venture, I have developed a set of 10 commonalities of suicide (Shneidman, 1985). I see these as phenomenologically self-evident, and I find these psychological characteristics in every case (historical or current) that I look at, because I have the capacity to translate every instance into those terms. The 10 commonalities are as follows:

1. The common *purpose* of suicide is to seek a solution.

2. The common *goal* of suicide is the cessation of consciousness—the unbearable flow of intolerable mind content.

3. The common *stimulus* in suicide is intolerable psychological pain. Every suicide can be understood in terms of pain—unbearable psychological pain, idiosyncratically defined.

4. The common *stressor* in suicide is frustrated psychological needs. In Henry Murray's (1983), *Explorations in Personality*, we have served to us, on a golden platter, an explication of some 30 psychological needs. It is thwarting or blocking of certain needs—critical in the makeup of *that* individual—that causes the pain that pushes the suicide. I believe that it is necessary to understand this need system in order to understand an individual case of suicide.

5. The common *emotion* in suicide is helplessness-hopelessness. This seems not only evident from developmental psychology, but also avoids the unnecessary sibling rivalry among the relevant emotions: guilt, shame, fear, and Stekel's hostility.

6. The common *cognitive state* in suicide is ambivalence. The pervasive presence of wanting to stop unbearable pain and wanting to survive in a state of less pain—in other words, ambivalence—is universally documented.

7. The common *perceptual state* in suicide is constriction. One has to be mindful of and deal with that word "only": "the only thing I could do"; "the only way to commit suicide." Dealing with constriction is a first order of preventional business.

8. The common *action* in suicide is egression. There are ways of substituting more benign egressions or blocking the exits, including getting the gun.

9. The common *interpersonal act* in suicide is communication of intention. Not secrecy or withdrawal, but communication, albeit in code, is the hallmark of committed suicide.

10. The common *consistency* in suicide is with lifelong coping patterns. Individuals are enormously loyal to themselves and their own armamentaria, even (or especially) in their dying. This is seen in a careful examination of an anamnestic record in the nuances of egressions (e.g., leaving home, quitting a job, ending a marriage, etc.).

This compilation has been further refined into a theoretical model. In its schematic form, it is a suicidal cube (see Figure 1-1). The three surfaces of the cube are labeled "pain," "perturbation" (consisting of constriction and a penchant for precipitous action), and "press." "Press," from positive to negative, is Murray's (1938) term for everything that is done to an individual before (or to which) he or she responds. It

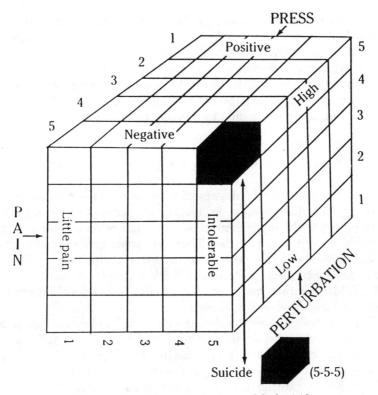

Figure 1-1. A theoretical cubic model of suicide.

includes DNA, parents, siblings, school, events, and chance. In this model, the suicidal cubelet (blackened in the figure) is in the right-hand corner, indicating the maximum concatenation of pain, perturbation, and (negative) press.

The implications for research would seem to be endless: to make comparisons, from the general (nonsuicidal) literature of psychiatry and psychology (perception, memory, learning, etc.) between and among pain and perturbation, pain and press, and press and perturbation, including their near-synonyms. All it takes is a careful, scholarly examination of the entire professional literature—a task that I am on the threshold of beginning.

The implications of this cubic model for treatment would seem to be obvious: Reduce (in reality or by reconceptualizing) the psychological pain a bit, and/or widen the opportunities for choice, and/or constrain the proclivity for irreversible action, and/or diminish the negative press. That is the utterly straightforward and relatively simple way in which lives can be saved: Mollify the pain, the perturbation, or the negative press. No one commits suicide in a nonsuicidal combination.

Suicidology within the Larger Social Setting

I turn now to the second category of my reflections—specifically, the changing place of suicidology within the also-changing social matrix. I have reflected about the impact of social policy on suicide acts and on suicide prevention activities. There are some generalizations that one can make about suicide and public policy in this country. In this, I am following the lead of Professor Shirley Zimmermann at the University of Minnesota in her recent book on family policy (Zimmermann, 1988). Four hypotheses are offered:

1. The more identifiable the risk, the more closely targeted the public (and legislative) response to relieve it will be. Thus it follows that suicidologists have a clear responsibility to identify, delineate, and disseminate (in ordinary language) the common clues to suicide.

2. The more organized and intense the political activity on behalf of potential victims, the more likely it is that public policy will concern itself with that problem. In this regard, it makes good tactical sense for us to focus on certain targeted groups, such as suicide among the young.

3. The more elevated the status of the potential victims (i.e., if it is likely to touch *us*), the more intense the public policy response will be, and vice versa. In this country today, we are only now becoming sufficiently alarmed about AIDS (acquired immune deficiency syndrome) because we realize that it is more than a malady of the "four H's": homosexuals, Haitians, hemophiliacs, and heroin addicts. It is because we fear that the disease may jump out of the containment of these groups and involve ordinary and "good citizens" that concern about AIDS is becoming widespread. In suicide, also, we are not egalitarian about death; we mourn the suicide of the talented, the beautiful, or the young more than that of the untalented, the homely, or the old. Here again, it is a stategic point to place an emphasis on youth suicide prevention and the use of young spokespersons. Nor is there anything nefarious in reciting these social realities.

4. The more congruent the prevention strategies are with current political and policy trends, the more active the political and policy response on that topic will be. Here especially, there are some palpable changes to be seen in this country over the past 40 years.

It gives me no pleasure to report that there are, in fact, fairly solid cross-sectional empirical data on this last topic. A systematic study of the 50 states of the United States, in a study done by Zimmermann (1988) using 1980 and 1982 total data, correlated the amounts of expenditures for education and public service programs with suicide rates and teenage birth rates, state by state. The results clearly demonstrate a statistically significant *negative* correlation between per capita state public welfare expenditures and suicide: The lower the expenditure for public welfare within the state, the higher the suicide rate; the more generous the expenditure, the lower the suicide rate. Obviously one of the things needed is more than a modicum of government (both state and federal) support to effect a truly meaningful reduction in suicidal deaths.

Since the 1940s, when I first turned to (and then never turned away from) the joint topics of suicide and suicide prevention, I have been a suicidologist in this glorious country under the administration of nine presidents: Roosevelt, Truman, Eisenhower, Kennedy, Johnson, Nixon, Ford, Carter, and Reagan. It seems clear enough to me that more liberal federal leaderships tend in general to tolerate and support a variety of approaches, including sociological and psychological approaches, to what we call our social problems, including suicide; conversely, more conservative federal leadership—on a generally *reduced* overall level, specifically in the case of suicide—tends to emphasize biological and medical solutions, with the implied locus of blame in the person rather than in the social structure, and thus tends to cut down on the necessary catholicity of approaches.

One insufficiently recognized culture hero in America is Jonas Salk. If there has been a swing in this country in suicidology in the last 30 years, it has been from Freud to Salk: Biologicize the problem, concentrate on one disease, find the virus, and develop the vaccine—that is the current American way. This is an unarguably marvelous solution when one is dealing with *infantile* paralysis, but it is a model that in all likelihood is not applicable if one is dealing with a case of *hysterical* paralysis. And who is to say that suicide, paradigmatically speaking, is not more like the latter than the former? I finally believe that suicide is not a disease; it is, rather, a bio-socio-psycho-philosophical malaise.

A sad but curious fact is that the same people who talk about prayer in our schools—which seems clearly unconstitutional as I understand that noble document—also want to practice a flawed form of social Darwinism toward the less advantaged, in which a crisis or failure (e.g., suicide) is seen as the individual's own fault, and in which the larger group, sociobiologically speaking, might well be rid of that unadapting individual. At its heart, this attitude is opposed to suicide prevention. We are well advised to believe that this anachronistic 19th-century frontier philosophy imposed on a late 20th-century complex society is too costly for good conscience.

One obvious conclusion to draw from all this is that the *dramatis personae* along the Potomac are indeed keenly relevant to our public policies and the resulting suicide prevention programs that flow from them—both their magnitude and their nature—as they filter down to the states and cities. In relation to suicide prevention, I am convinced that we must wait until 1989, after the next presidential inauguration, for any really meaningful action to be effected.

Ernest Hilgard's (1986) recent comprehensive volume, *Psychology in America*, contains a chapter subheading that has caught my attention: "Topics that Become Centers of Excitement." Although he does not discuss suicide, in my mind that is what the suicide prevention movement has been in America: a topic that has become a center of excitement. For honesty's sake, I need to add that I did not quote Hilgard's subheading in its entirety. It is actually "Topics that Become Centers of Excitement over a Short Time Span." I hope that this is not going to be true for the suicide prevention movement or for the AAS, and I have reasons to believe that it will not be so, although certain subinterests (e.g., the current tactical focus on youth suicide) may very well wax and wane over the next few years.

Our broader hope is that the general concern with suicide prevention across the board, having been established, will endure. But I believe that this endurance will not happen on its own, and that we must all work to see that new conceptualizations, decent research efforts (both nomethetic and idiographic), and informed training programs ensure the continuance of suicidology. These are a few of my reflections about suicide, suicide prevention, the AAS over the 1968–1988 interval, and its role for the rest of this century. I hope that readers have found these remarks either interesting or provocative, preferably both.

Remarks from 1968 AAS Meeting

I now have the pleasure of quoting some very special, albeit brief remarks made at the first meeting of the AAS in 1968. Here are their voices, expressing various points of view.

Jacques Choron: "Not sufficient attention has been paid to the difference between the death of another person, even of a loved one, and what I could call my own death. My death is something entirely different than the death of another person. A therapist who deals with a potentially suicidal patient or who is talking about the notions of death of the patient may help to re-establish communication between the patient and the therapist. It may also have diagnostic value in the sense that it may help us to establish the lethality of the patient."

Lawrence Kubie: "And finally as an act of desperation they slash their wrists a little bit, sometimes accidentally going too deep; they take whatever drugs they happen to have on hand; and they must all come into our statistics on suicide. But what the patient is trying to do is save his life. Many acts of self-injury which are lumped together under the concept of suicide do not have self-extinction as their goal."

Erwin Stengel: "The psychoanalytic contribution to suicide research has been mainly concerned with the intrapsychic dynamics of self-destructive tendencies. This has been both its strength and its limitation. It has until recently not concerned itself with the external world, apart from those objects which by introjection become parts of the inner world. Zilboorg's discovery of the role of the broken home in suicide proneness was a brilliant observation deduced from the study of intrapsychic processes and confirmed by clinical and epidemiological studies."

Louis Dublin: "The lay volunteer was probably the most important single discovery in the 50-year history of suicide prevention. Little progress was made until he came into the picture, for he alone apparently was qualified to make the live and fruitful contacts with the person in distress. He had the time and the qualities of character to prove that he cared. With proper training he can make a successful approach to the client. He can through direct friendly contact discover the principal cause of his difficulties and by his knowledge of the community services which are available for useful referral, he can often tide his client over his crisis."

Karl Menninger: "I think that it is important to distinguish between suicide as a form of death and suicide as an attempt at expression of something within one—helplessness, desperation, fear, the other emotions. The organism says, 'Anything rather than suicide; anything rather than have to give up the most precious thing of all—namely, my life. Sickness, yes, even neurosis, even crime, but not that awful oblivion, that awful ultimate nothingness.' The suicidal gesture is thus a cry not only of distress, not only a cry for help, not only a prayer, one might say, but it is a pleading: 'I want to live; help me to find a way to live.'"

Concluding Remarks

My final remarks are purely personal reflections. The nature of my childhood and then later of my being a parent conspired together to give me a certain psychodynamic orientation toward living systems. Thus, it was quite natural for me to view the AAS as a child of mine. I delight in having sired it; I am fiercely proud of what it has become; and I am entirely happy now to have it live on, unencumbered by any unnecessary meddling by me. It seems the natural thing to do: to give a living system—a little human being, a group, a center, or an association—the breath of life and then, after an appropriate period of devoted nurturing, to let it have an independent existence (with, of course, never-ending strings of concern and love, but not of control). This has been my life in suicidology. I have found it worth living, and would gladly live it again if the chance were offered me.

References

Aaron, D. (Ed.). *The Inman diary: A public and private confession.* (Vols. 1 and 2). Cambridge, MA: Harvard University Press, 1985.

Aries, P. *The hour of our death.* New York: Knopf, 1981. (Originally published, 1977.)

Friedman, P. (Ed.). *On suicide.* New York: International Universities Press, 1967.

Hilgard, E. *Psychology in America: A historical survey.* San Diego, CA: Harcourt Brace Jovanovich, 1987.

Iga, M. *The thorn in the chrysanthemum: Suicide and economic success in modern Japan.* Berkeley and Los Angeles: University of California Press, 1986.

Murray, H. A. *Explorations in personality.* New York: Oxford University Press, 1983.

Shneidman, E. S. *Definition of suicide.* New York: Wiley, 1985.

Zimmermann, S. *Understanding family policy.* Newbury Park, CA: Sage, 1988.

CHAPTER 2

Founder's Perspectives—Then and Now

Erwin Ringel, MD
Medical School, University of Vienna

In 1948 I was permitted to establish a suicide prevention center in Vienna as part of CARITAS, an organization within the Catholic Church. Vienna's bishops initially tended toward the idea that I would have to teach the center's clients to be good Catholics. The problem would then be solved, since it would be forbidden for good Catholics to kill themselves. When I was not willing to work in such a fashion, the bishops showed great tolerance and said, "Go your own way." This involved building up a team consisting of psychiatrists, psychotherapists, social workers, lawyers, and spiritual advisors; later, when Hans Hoff became its chairman, close cooperation with the Psychiatric Clinic was included as well. In 1960 we were of the opinion that we had gathered enough experience to be able to share it with other similar institutions. Therefore, in the summer of that year we convened, in Vienna, the first European conference on suicide prevention. When I discovered the lively exchange of thoughts between the different countries at the conference to be so stimulating, I had the idea of creating an international association for suicide prevention. With the support of all the pioneers in our field, especially those from the United States, I succeeded in actually realizing this idea on a worldwide scale. I believe that this event was unique, insofar as at that time there were no national associations for suicide prevention in existence. In almost every other scientific field there had first of all been national associations, from which gradually an international association had emerged to act as an umbrella organization, binding together all the national associations. In our case it was the reverse.

Is an International Association Still Necessary?

As the founder of the International Association for Suicide Prevention (IASP), I now have a question to answer today—one that I naturally have asked myself every year since 1960. Is an international association still necessary when so many national associations already exist and, happily, when new ones are constantly in the process of being set up? I have to ask whether suicide prevention includes tasks that absolutely require an international basis. I would once again like to answer this question with an emphatic "yes," and give my reasons as follows.

Suicide Prevention as a World View

First, one could call suicide prevention a form of world view, and even this word contains the world as a concept that pushes beyond the borders of individual countries and continents. Of course, in different countries there are different attitudes to the suicide problem. Therefore, because of this, there is also the duty (I use the word in the sense of a generally obligatory humanitarianism) to advocate worldwide certain attitudes to the problem of suicide. The glorification of suicide as the greatest act of human courage must be combated as much as condemnation of suicide must be. Also, indifference to this problem, in which it is a question of deciding between life and death, cannot be the right solution.

It may seem perhaps strange that I, as someone who tries to prevent suicide, emphasize here that the right of human beings to kill themselves by their own hands cannot be denied them. Humans are the only living creatures who, on the one hand, know that their existence is limited and, on the other hand, have recognized that they can end their own lives themselves. It would be as much unrealistic as inhuman to deny them this possibility. But it would be just as inhuman not to insure that all those who are in dire need—and this accounts for practically all suicides—are extended a helping hand to help them get over their crises. In the United States, a very good slogan was recently created: "Suicide is an eternal solution for what is often merely a temporary problem." This sentence indicates a recognition of the importance of the time factor in suicide. Many people who commit suicide would judge their situation, only a short time later, quite differently from the way they did at the time of the act—if they still had an opportunity to do so. Of course there are always going to be people who cannot be helped, even in the long term, not even with the improved means of present-day medical, psychological, and social therapy. But happy the person who can be told what the great writer Heinrich von Kleist told his sister shortly before his suicide: "I very much want to confirm to you that you did everything that was humanly possible to keep me alive. The truth, however, is that I was not to be helped in this world."

It is the job of an international association to do everything possible so that the commitment to help others increases in the world and so that the words of Hölderlin come true as much as possible everywhere: "Where there is danger, that which saves grows with it." It is unfortunately a sad and indisputable fact that danger is growing, including the danger of suicide and the fact that no country remains untouched by it.

Suicide Prevention for the Oppressed

In this connection, it is necessary to put through a second point of view worldwide. Before the majesty of the law—in this case, the law governing suicide prevention—all human beings are truly equal. It is precisely the despised, those people upon whom society heaps contempt, who are in particular need of special prophylactic treatment, because it is they who are particularly endangered. The crucial principle of suicide prevention, after all, is that each individual life is important. The aim of suicide prevention is not so much to reduce the suicide rates, after all, but to help people—to make it possible for each individual person to take the road of self-realization rather than that of failure, of which the final consequence is suicide. We cannot value different people in different ways; each human life is equally valuable. There are no superhuman and no subhuman beings; there are in fact human beings to whom one feels "incorrigibly drawn," as Morgenstern put it, and to whom one offers one's hand.

There can unfortunately be no doubt that those people in most danger of committing suicide come from groups who have been driven into assuming the role of outsiders and the persecuted. Let us not forget those people (and unfortunately their names are legion in our times) who are persecuted for reasons of race, religion, or politics. May I, as an Austrian—who in this regard, and also because of more recent tragic election results in my country, finds himself in a difficult position—point to the persecution that the Jews had to suffer during the Nazi period? During the period 1933–1945, the rate of Jewish suicides increased heavily under the pressure of Nazi persecution. The persecution of the Jews is the most conspicuous, perhaps, but certainly only one of many examples. Suicide prevention efforts must be particularly aware of the kinds of situations that arise under oppression of this sort, especially since the ruling powers tend to prohibit any kind of assistance for the endangered group.

Who would want to disagree that such and other similar problems do not go far beyond national horizons and call for international humanitarianism? Thus worldwide responsibility will always be necessary in order to recognize that in a particular society people are essentially condemned to suicide or driven to suicide—in other words, must suffer tragic death at their own hands, and this neither freely nor voluntarily. Just as no man is an island, as John Donne once said, it is also true that no human being is a state, and we are all required not to let the endangered person down.

I would like to mention yet another example in this connection, which can only lead to a pleasing result on an international basis. In the countries behind the Iron Curtain, it was formerly believed that every suicide was a protest against society. Thanks to a persistent presentation of our scientific discoveries in the Eastern bloc, which showed that very individual problems also play a role, often on a psychopathological basis, attitudes to suicide went through a fundamental change. This also included directly setting up measures to prevent suicide. The majority of these countries are now members of the IASP.

Dissemination of Findings

Another remark I want to make leads on to a further task that can only be carried out on an international basis. I mean the dissemination of findings as regards the prevention of suicide, both in the scientific area and in the practical, institutionalized area. Information here can be of decisive importance on the one hand, and on the other can serve as the basis for a fundamental exchange of experiences, which can lead to the confirmation or modification of prophylactic measures or to their rejection. The dialogue between one country and the next and among all countries adds both to the theory and to the practice of suicide prevention; were this dialogue not to take place, we would walk in parallel, oblivious of our isolation and at the same time having to fend for ourselves.

I would like to mention just one example for each of the areas I referred to earlier: for the scientific area, international experience of presuicidal syndrome; for the sociopolitical area, the extremely important change that the attitude of the Roman Catholic Church toward the problem of suicide has undergone in the past decade. It almost ought to be called a sensation that those who commit suicide no longer appear among those persons who are to be denied a religious burial, according to the new code book of the Catholic Church. It is, however, in this connection, a very strange fact that the Church has virtually prevented this change from becoming public knowledge, although everyone can read it in the *Codex Juris Canonici*. Even the majority of priests are not aware of this. In such a situation, it becomes evident that an international association is precisely what is required to make such an occurence known on a wider basis.

As far as the institutional problems are concerned, I would like to use this opportunity to point out once again that in 1970 the Austrian government recognized that suicide prevention is a duty of society and thus of the state. As a consequence of this recognition, the private CARITAS suicide prevention center in Vienna was reorganized on a new basis, in which the state also participates accordingly. One cannot repeat this often enough on an international level, with the hope that this example will finally be followed. It would also be desirable to at least create, at long last, a Day of Suicide Prevention, so that it can be made clear on a wider basis how many people who are in great need or have been abandoned find death at their own hands—a death that one can regard, as many writers have done, as the most tragic end that a human life can experience.

International Comparative Studies

Many problems of suicide prevention demand comparative studies from country to country. As a perfect example in this connection, one could mention the study that the unforgetable Erwin Stengel carried out together with Norman Farberow. In this case, it was a question of the basis on which suicide statistics in each country are compiled. In the process it was possible to prove, tragically, that the prerequisites differ completely from country to country, meaning that we compare figures with a relatively high degree of reliability with those of lower reliability, and thus compare the incomparable.

To continue, I would like to mention three further problems here, which can only be reasonably clarified by international comparative examination. I mean (1) the basis for a psychologically sound climate that does not encourage suicide; (2) the principles of an upbringing that will make people less susceptible to suicide than is now the case; and (3) especially the urgent question of whether and how it is possible to report about suicide in the media in such fashion that any external influence, and the danger of this becoming epidemic, can be excluded. Only recently, Häfner and Schmidtke demonstrated in a solidly based study that a very accurately produced (i.e., as accurately produced as present-day knowledge allows) television series about the death of a schoolboy in the subway led tragically to a significant increase in the number of suicides among young people, which were committed in the same fashion. Our dear friend Jerome Motto proved a long time ago that the suicide figures in Detroit fell in a period when no papers appeared because of a strike. Abolishing newspapers cannot be the solution to the problem, however, and making the problem of suicide a taboo subject in the media would not bring us very far either. We must therefore humbly admit that we still have no solution to this problem at the present moment, and that it will require the best minds in all countries to come up with something new that will be of practical use.

General problems in the world—to name a few, misery; hunger; homelessness; social injustice; lack of hygiene; epidemics; population explosions; dealing with the handicapped, the elderly, and the unemployed; drug use; armaments; and pollution—are of course closely connected with the prevention of suicide. The World Health Organization, in its program "Health for All by the Year 2000," sees overcoming these problems as the most important of common goals, but of course in countries in which not even naked survival is assured for the majority of the steadily growing population, these cannot even begin to be of topical importance. It will of course also be clear to everyone that remedies in these areas can only be provided by international cooperation *and* solidarity, and that only the greatest of effort from everyone, particularly from the fully industrialized nations, can bring results.

Concluding Remarks

I could continue to discuss problems that exist in connection with suicide prevention, and that can only be solved on an international basis, at considerably greater length. I hope, however, that these remarks of mine will suffice to make everyone understand that in the field of suicide prevention not only are national associations necessary, but an international one is an absolute necessity.

We have had a sad experience, which I cannot begin to conceal here. Since the founding in many countries of national organizations (which we have always strongly encouraged), we are of course getting no new members from these countries. Thus the IASP is forced to lead only a modest existence, as far as membership and thereby also the financial base are concerned. We now have 225 individual members and a budget of approximately $7,000 (U.S. dollars) a year. It will be clear to everyone that we cannot take great strides forward with that. Unfortunately, it must be said that none of the national associations have shown any great interest in the fate of the IASP. The fact that we organize a world congress every other year is thankfully acknowledged, but more or less according to the motto, "God helps those who help themselves." Perhaps we should (but we will not as long as I and my fellow disciple Dr. Sonneck are still alive) say that the IASP is in a presuicidal situation. Perhaps, then, the national associations would come to our aid and remember their duty.

I do not want, however, to overlook the possibility that the cloud may have a silver lining, and, as the fellow disciple of Alfred Adler, would like to end this speech with this hope. I would like to thank the whole executive board of the American Association of Suicidology (AAS) and, in particular, our vice-president Charlotte Ross, for the joint meeting of the IASP and the AAS that has taken place. Perhaps this is the beginning of true cooperation between national and international associations.

CHAPTER 3

In Remembrance of Things Past: Prospects for the Future

Cynthia R. Pfeffer, MD
Cornell University Medical College

The Chilean Nobel laureate poet, Pablo Neruda, once asked, *"Porqué se suicidan las hojas cuando se sienten amarillas?"* ("Why do leaves commit suicide when they feel yellow?") (1981, p. 10). In this metaphor, Neruda ponders one of the most profound issues of human existence: Why does one commit suicide? By implication, his metaphor suggests that there are developmental, life-phase-specific determinants and perhaps biological origins of suicide. His metaphor captures the universality of the condition. It transcends culture, yet it is associated with intent arising from specific conditions. The phenomenon is observable by many; however, it is actually fully appreciated by relatively few. It is this last remark that I wish to emphasize.

In this volume commemorating the historic first joint meeting of the American Association of Suicidology (AAS) and the International Association for Suicide Prevention (IASP), we share our convergent and divergent views. My message is that we have accumulated many data about the phenomenon of suicide, but that they have been sometimes underutilized, sometimes forgotten, and sometimes never sufficiently highlighted. Many past observations, while requiring continued and additional validation, should form the basis for our current and future work efforts. It is my premise that we must retain past knowledge, integrate it, and reassess our current perspectives and emphasis on our quest to understand and respond to the needs of suicide prevention.

Since my main orientation as a child psychiatrist is toward youth, I have chosen to discuss concepts by means of illustrations that focus on children and adolescents. In fact, this choice is quite compatible with international and national efforts to understand youth suicidal behavior in the last several years. In actuality, these illustrations are good representatives of suicidal phenomena for all ages.

This paper was given as the Presidential Address for the AAS, San Francisco, May 1987.

Features of Suicidal Behaviors

Suicidal behavior is a complex, multidetermined phenomenon that can be understood from a variety of key vantage points: psychosocial, sociocultural, constitutional–biological, and many others. The short story "Paul's Case" (Cather, 1905/1956) highlights many of the psychosocial features of suicide. Paul was a tall, thin adolescent attending Pittsburgh High School at the time he was suspended from school. Many wondered whether he had abused drugs. He "was quite accustomed to lying; [he] found it, indeed, indispensable for overcoming friction.... Disorder and impertinence were among the offences named [by the school], yet each of his instructors felt that it was scarcely possible to put into words the real cause of the trouble" (p. 150). Paul was asked to appear before the school faculty to account for his actions before he could return to school. The faculty was ruthless toward him:

[Paul] stood through it smiling.... Older boys than Paul had broken down and shed tears under that ordeal ... His teachers were in despair, and his drawing teacher voiced the feeling of them all when he declared that there was something about the boy which none of them understood. He added: "I don't really believe that smile of his comes altogether from insolence; there's something sort of haunted about it. The boy is not strong, for one thing. There is something wrong about the fellow." (pp. 150–151)

In contrast to the opinions of the school faculty, Paul was a much-liked usher at the local music hall. "Nothing was too much trouble for him; he carried messages and brought programs as though it were his greatest pleasure in life, and all the people in his section called him a charming boy, feeling that he remembered and admired them" (p. 153). However, family life was barren for him. He could not remember his mother and he hardly interacted with his father. In fact, it was at the music hall and the local theatre "that Paul really lived; the rest was but a sleep and a forgetting. This was Paul's fairy tale, and it had for him all the allurement of a secret love.... After a night behind the scenes, Paul found the schoolroom more than ever repulsive" (pp. 161–162).

The situation got increasingly worse for Paul at school until he was permanently suspended. His father put Paul to work. The manager at the music hall and the doorkeeper at the theatre were told not to admit him. His good friend promised Paul's father that he would not see him. In a short time, Paul decided to leave town. He stole money he was delivering to the bank for a business company. With this, he set out for New York City: "It had been wonderfully simple; when they had shut him out of the theatre and concert hall, when they had taken away his bone, the whole thing was virtually determined.... Until

now, he could not remember a time when he had not been dreading
something. . . . But now he had a curious sense of relief" (p. 166).

Once in New York, he checked into the Waldorf and began to tour
the city. "He could not remember a time when he had felt so at peace
with himself. The mere release from the necessity of petty lying, lying
every day and every day, restored his self-respect" (p. 170). Several
days after his arrival in New York, Paul read in the Pittsburgh newspapers a description of what he had done. His father was reportedly
coming East to bring him home. "It was to be worse than jail" (p. 171).
The next day,

[Paul] rose and moved about with painful effort. . . . It was the old depression exaggerated. . . . yet somehow he was not afraid of anything, was absolutely calm; perhaps
because he had looked into the dark corner at last, and knew. . . . He saw everything
clearly now. . . . for half an hour he sat staring at the revolver. But he told himself that
was not the way, so he went downstairs and took a cab to the ferry. When Paul arrived
at Newark, he got off the train and took another cab, directing the driver to follow the
Pennsylvania tracks out of the town. (p. 173)

Paul dismissed the cab and walked along the train tracks, thinking.
"His mind, unable to cope with vital matters near at hand, worked
feverishly and deftly at sorting and grouping these images. They made
for him a part of the ugliness of the world" (p. 173). Eventually, he
stopped walking and slept for a while.

The sound of an approaching train woke him, and he started to his feet, remembering
only his resolution, and afraid lest he should be too late. He stood watching the approaching
locomotive, his teeth chattering, his lips drawn away from them in a frightened smile;
once or twice he glanced nervously sidewards, as though he were being watched. When
the right moment came, he jumped. As he fell, the folly of his haste occurred to him
with merciless clearness, the vastness of what he had left undone. (p. 174)

This remarkably lucid description of the travails of a suicidal teenager
is supported by recent research on suicidal youth. Intense and chronic
depression with antisocial features, and a sense of isolation from family
and social milieu, are prominent factors in the histories of suicidal
youths (Pfeffer, 1986a). The suicidal episode—appearing impulsive, at
the time, with a general degree of constricted thinking, but actually
planned, rehearsed, and effectively carried out by a lethal method—
has been the hallmark of numerous adolescent suicides (Shaffer, 1974;
Shafii, Carrigan, Whittinghall, & Derrick, 1985). Finally, the fact that
this extensive description was written in 1905 by Willa Cather, an
esteemed American author, emphasizes my basic premise that much
has been observed and understood about the motives and psychosocial
determinants of youth suicidal behavior long before our "rediscovery"

of this phenomenon during recent times, when youth suicide rates have so extensively increased.

An example of sociocultural factors for suicide has been incisively documented in the detailed personal observations and reminiscences of Thomas Bernhard in his book *Gathering Evidence* (1985). This noted Austrian writer described his experiences at the age of 13 in Salzburg in the 1940s, when he was haunted by his student life at a boarding school and by the war. In thinking about his situation at the boarding school, he remembered (writing of himself in the third person) that

nobody explained to him that it is necessary for his education, and he can only feel betrayed. . . . Absolute obedience and subordination are required of the pupils, the subordination of the weak to the strong . . . enduring increasingly severe punishment, which in the end produces utter hopelessness. . . . It is in the very nature of things that the main thought which occupies his mind during the first few days is *the thought of suicide* . . . by jumping out a window or hanging himself. . . . He actually made many suicide attempts . . . but they were never carried *too far.* (pp. 79–81)

Bernhard observed, "Many boys actually did commit suicide at the boarding house. . . . They all threw themselves out of windows in the dormitory or the lavatories or hanged themselves from the showers in the washroom" (p. 82). He observed on "the suicide street" the bodies of many schoolchildren.

Bernhard, as an adolescent, had a curious concept of the act of suicide; for him it was an act requiring strength, decisiveness, or firmness of character. He suggested, "It is probably true that in boarding establishments, especially those with exceedingly sadistic regimes and exceedingly bad climactic conditions . . . the subject which occupies the minds of the pupils is suicide" (pp. 82–83). With regard to his own experiences, Bernhard wrote, "The idea of suicide and the phenomenon of suicide were continually debated, but always *in silence.* And again, and again, we had a real suicide in our midst" (p. 83). Bernhard had particular ideas about suicide that were specific to young people. He suggested, "Those most liable to suicide have always been the young: young people who have been passed off by parents and guardians and sent away to learn and to study, but who spend their time brooding upon self-extinction and self-annihilation—young people for whom everything is still true and real and who come to grief because the truth and the reality are too terrible to bear" (p. 84).

The sociocultural factors so much discussed in regard to youth suicide in recent decades are not so dissimilar to the factors Thomas Bernhard experienced and highlighted. The character of the educational system, where youngsters spend most of their time, is clearly molded by sociocultural influences. At the extreme where untoward effects are prevalent is an atmosphere of dehumanization, excessive academic and/or social pressures, traits that disempower youth rights, and excessive autonomy and loneliness. Bernhard captured the occurrence of clusters of suicides with their contagion and imitative effects. Certainly, loss of family supports, with an intense sense of parental betrayal, is a factor observed by others (Pfeffer, 1986b) in regard to youth suicide. Finally, the brutality and violence of certain societal situations must be regarded as important factors for a high rate of suicide among youths. Surely, if we contemplate the types of experiences described by Bernhard and relate them to our current concerns about sociocultural and global determinants of suicidal behavior, we cannot be considering these issues for the first time.

Biological underpinnings of suicidal behavior have been more difficult to define. In fact, there are many levels on which biological factors have an impact on suicidal risk. The following example of a preadolescent points out the interactions among individual psychology, family conflict, and some type of biological influence. In the short story "The Rocking-Horse Winner" (Lawrence, 1926/1983), Paul was a perceptive young English child who sensed conflicts in his home. There was an overriding feeling that his mother could not love her children. Furthermore, although the parents and the three children "lived in style, they felt always an anxiety in the house. There was never enough money. . . . And so the house came to be haunted by the unspoken phrase: *there must be more money!*" (pp. 790–791). In a conversation one day with his mother, Paul found out that his mother had a meaningful feeling about luck. She said, "It's what causes you to have money. If you're lucky you have money. That's why it's better to be born lucky than rich. If you're rich, you may lose your money. But, if you're lucky, you will always get more money" (p. 792). Paul immediately explained that he was a lucky person: "God told me" (p. 792).

Paul spent much time on his big rocking horse, "charging madly into space . . . When he had ridden to the end of his mad little journey . . . he would silently command the snorting steed, 'Now, take me where there is luck!'" (p. 793). Paul, befriended by his uncle and several others who liked horse races, bet regularly. When Paul placed bets, he nearly always won; the others were amazed. Paul saved his money to give to his mother. His reason was that his mother told him that she had no luck. "I thought if *I* was lucky, it might stop whispering. . . . I *hate* our house for whispering. . . . like people laughing at you behind your back. It's awful, that is!" (p. 798). Unbeknownst to her, Paul gave his mother his money on her birthday. But this amount was not satisfactory. "The voices in the house suddenly went mad . . . and screamed in a sort of ecstasy: 'There *must* be more money! . . . More than ever!' It frightened Paul terribly. . . . He became wild-eyed and strange, as if something were going to explode in him. . . . I've got to know for the Derby!' " (p. 800).

Two nights before the Epsom Derby, Paul mounted his wooden rocking horse to get the answer about which horse would be the winner. He rode and rode in a frenzied state with his mother watching in anxious disbelief. " 'It's Malabar!' he screamed . . . as he ceased urging his wooden horse. Then he fell with a crash to the ground . . . But he was unconscious, and unconscious he remained with some brain-fever. . . . The third day of the illness was critical . . . He neither slept nor regained consciousness" (pp. 803–804). The race took place. Paul's friend, the gardener, raced into the room to tell Paul the news that he had placed a bet for Paul on Malabar and that he had won a large sum of money. Upon hearing this, Paul explained, "I never told you, mother, that if I can ride my horse, and *get there*, then I'm absolutely sure—oh, absolutely! Mother, did I ever tell you? I *am* lucky!" (p. 804). Paul died that night.

Although this story does not directly depict suicidal behavior, this elegant depiction by D. H. Lawrence in "The Rocking-Horse Winner" of a young child's preoccupations that eventually led to compulsive self-destructive behaviors suggests that they were related to the family dynamics. An inference is that the child's psychosis and eventual death had an organic component, diagnosed as "brain-fever." Such a diagnosis was appropriate in the early 20th century, when there was less scientific knowledge about the biological basis of brain functions. Nevertheless, scientific advances in research methodology have suggested a type of "brain-fever" among certain suicidal individuals who, for example, have been found to be deficient in brain neurotransmitter metabolites of serotonin (van Praag, 1986). Other research suggests that neuroendocrine, neurotransmitter, and genetic factors are associated with some individuals' suicidal behavior.

Prospects for the Future

Advances in modern technology have opened up new possibilities for the prevention of suicide; at the same time, they have also created new stresses. Our endeavors require an increased use of the positive aspects of these advances. At the same time, much is known about suicidal behavior, but has not been disseminated or accepted sufficiently. We have a rich heritage from the past and much to look forward to in the future. In fact, knowledge about human motivations and behaviors involving suicidal behavior are reflected often in literature and other art forms. Many such depictions agree with the historic and scientific endeavors to integrate information relevant to suicidal behavior by

Sigmund Freud, Emile Durkheim, Louis Dublin, the 1910 Vienna psychoanalytic symposium on Suicide, the founders of the AAS and the IASP, and numerous others.

Prospectives for future work in suicidology must be broadened beyond what knowledge has been already accrued. This can be accomplished if we maintain a philosophy of flexibility, open-mindedness, curiosity, and aggressiveness to pursue new hypotheses and to make use of newly developed research techniques and innovative, practically based clinical approaches. Furthermore, our efforts must be organized in an intense spirit of collegiality and respect for differences in disciplines and orientations.

Specifically, domains of discourse must be evaluated by teams of experts trained in the complexities of specific psychosocial, biological, sociocultural, philosophical, and other relevant issues. Efforts in scientific investigations must go hand in hand with developing more effective practical applications for suicide prevention. In this way, the multifaceted components of suicidal behavior can be better understood. For example, the expressions of suicidal impulses among individuals need to be studied for their etiology, natural course, and treatment responses. In so doing, we may come to a better understanding of whether suicidal behavior is a distinct psychopathological entity, and, if so, whether it is a homogeneous or a heterogeneous one. Also, this will enable the development of more precise methods of prevention and intervention that may address early antecedent factors for suicidal behavior, rather than remediation of an already manifest pathological constellation.

From a sociocultural perspective, it is essential to characterize the social fabric of local communities, nations, and more global spheres, and to develop approaches to enhance beneficial effects and limit adverse trends. For example, the extensive impact of modern technology must be more systematically understood, and efforts must be made to enhance the quality of life that these advances have the potential to produce. The technology of travel and communication has been able to bring people, ideas, and news of events together more rapidly. Information exchange that can enhance individuals' knowledge must be carried out in ways that have benefit as well as a guarantee to limit adverse responses or reactions.

In keeping with this, there is no doubt that human motivations, affects, fantasies, cognitions, and acts are mediated by biological factors. It is no longer valid to negate the impact of biological components of risk for suicidal behavior. New research technologies used in medical investigation are to be welcomed as approaches to understanding suicidal behavior. Promising inroads that may be helpful for suicidology have been reported in basic cell-biological research that captures the functioning of neurotransmitters and the identification of genetic factors. Other technologies utilizing brain imaging may, some time in the near future, be applied to the study of suicidal individuals. At present, it seems that suicide is a uniquely human condition, but it may be possible someday to develop animal or computer models of the suicide-prone individual. In so doing, efforts at prevention may be more precisely specified, especially if basic precursors of suicidal behavior can be defined.

Finally, the joint meeting in 1987 of the AAS and the IASP, just 20 years after the founding of the AAS, has brought together a large number of people from around the world who represent individuals working in a myriad of disciplines. It is my hope that an outcome of this meeting will be to open new vistas that can define future progressive perspectives that are motivated by highly collaborative attitudes among us. It was an honor for me to welcome all the colleagues who attended this meeting. Perhaps we can begin our work by remembering the past as we move toward the future. Let us, together, ask Neruda's question: "Why do leaves commit suicide when they feel yellow?"

References

Bernhard, T. *Gathering evidence*. New York: Knopf, 1985.

Cather, W. Paul's case. In W. Cather, *Five stories*. New York: Vintage Books. 1956. (Originally published, 1905.)

Lawrence, D. H. The rocking-horse winner. In D. H. Lawrence, *The complete short stories* (Vol. 3). Harmondsworth, England: Penguin Books, 1983. (Originally published, 1926.)

Neruda, P. *Libro de las preguntas: Seix barral obras de Pablo Neruda*. Barcelona, Spain: Biblioteca Breve, 1981.

Pfeffer, C. R. *The suicidal child*. New York: Guilford Press, 1986. (a)

Pfeffer, C. R. *Family characteristics and support systems as risk factors for youth suicidal behavior*. Paper presented at the meeting of the Department of Health and Human Services Secretary's Task Force on Youth Suicide, Bethesda, Md., 1986. (b)

Shaffer, D. Suicide in childhood and early adolescence. *Journal of Child Psychology and Psychiatry*, 1974, *15*, 275–291.

Shafii, M., Carrigan, S., Whittinghall, J. R., & Derrick, A. Psychological autopsy of completed suicide in children and adolescents. *American Journal of Psychiatry*, 1985, *142*, 1061–1064.

van Praag, H. M. Affective disorders and aggression disorders: Evidence for a common biological mechanism. *Suicide and Life-Threatening Behavior*, 1986, *16*, 103–132.

CHAPTER 4

The Decision to Terminate One's Life: Psychoanalytic Thoughts on Suicide

Leo Rangell, MD
Los Angeles, California

As my contribution to this volume on the violent termination of one's own life, I keep cultural values, epidemiological factors, and national and international aspects as a background. From this backdrop, I move from the ground to the figure, from the culture to the individual, to the human being pathologically affected by his or her surround and acting into it. Continuing within the individual to the more focal intrapsychic aspects, I look first from the background history to the decision itself, to the moment of its execution—the start of the jump, the turning on of the gas, the pulling of the trigger, the act that completes the ending of the life.

Anyone moving out on a ledge to talk to a would-be jumper had better have at least an intuitive idea of the psychological aura into which he or she has been cast. The police officer, psychologist, friend, or stranger entering the drama at this crucial moment represents the object world to a person who, often for the first time in his or her life, occupies center stage. One need not and cannot have an informed knowledge of the psychodynamics that have led to this moment. But an effective identification, often born of and surprisingly present in crisis, cannot fail to be of help. External advice or exhortation when the suicidal intention has taken such hold is of no value because external objects have been devalued. The last thing one should show now is a tone of insincerity. Rescuers instinctively know and feel this.

My approach to this subject that rivets the attention, that commands intense and universal interest, is from the experience and vantage point of a psychoanalytic generalist. I do not speak from a special

Expanded version of plenary address at the combined meeting of the American Association of Suicidology and the International Association for Suicide Prevention, San Francisco, May 27, 1987.

interest, nor from having been involved in any controlled experiment or focused research on this specific subject, which might in fact result in a skewed, exaggerated, and especially highlighted view; rather, I speak by virtue of my general data base. From this vantage point, I look at the suicidal impulse, or wish, or fleeting thought, as it resides in the general psychology of the population. In an active general psychiatric practice of well-nigh 50 years, I have not had an experience with suicide that would enable me to make claim to being a specialist. Anyone who did would be inclined to cover it and hide his or her expertise. On the other hand, any long-time psychiatrist who has had no experience with suicide is like a surgeon or internist who has never had a patient die because they turn sicker patients away to others.

I have seen suicide and overseen it. Perhaps of more universal applicability, I have observed its aborted, controlled, and redirected forms in a huge sample of general psychopathology. Looking over nearly 50 years of daily, continuous practice, in which my patients and I operated at the psychic depths for what I once calculated as well over 100,000 hours of free associations, I would say in an overall way that suicide as a universal fantasy occupies a discernible but small place in mental life. I do not attempt to quantify, but hope to arrive at an impression of its importance by descriptive and dynamic exploration.

The Latent and Quantitative Quality of Suicide

As a bridge to my assertion that suicide is latent and quantitative, and that under certain circumstances it can become commonly operative, the experience comes to mind that is connoted to us by the name "Jonestown." This natural experiment of astonishing proportions has, in my opinion, never been sufficiently absorbed or its grim psychological lessons extracted. About 980 persons quietly administered a lethal dose of poison to themselves and their children (some 250 of them), with no compelling internal or external reason except loyalty to their leader and to each other. Surely there was no convergent past psychodynamic history in all these victims, as much as they were tied and united by this common external bond and condition. What the act gave testament to was the power of followership, passivity, submission to charisma, and identifications upward and laterally (to the leader and to peers); the universal "need to belong" was not given up even at this price.

That such pathological behavior is not limited to ardent and overt cultists, but can affect a wider-based "normal" population, can be reflected upon and validated by an even worse example of submission to authority—in this instance, complying with aggression outward rather than toward the self. I am referring to the experience of another gripping "natural" experiment in our lifetime—this one of an entire nation, and more than one nation, passively enduring and permitting (if not actively participating in) genocide and torture. These two grim "natural" experiments did not need the official and more academic experiment performed by Milgram (1975) at Yale on "obedience to authority" to confirm these conclusions. These two polar examples—phenomenological manifestations of mass behavior in the service of genocide and suicide—are linked to the theoretical concept of the aggressive instinct, directed outward in one instance, and turned toward the self in the other. As an empirical observation that ties the two together, about one-third of all homicides include suicide.

To trace and understand the origins and vicissitudes of what can be called suicidal content in general psychology, one has to take into account gradations, structural aspects, and the developmental progression of mental constructs. In suicide, perhaps more than with any other mental content, the distance between the conscious intention offered verbally and what actions and attitudes reveal about more significant unconscious intention is a crucial datum for explanation and understanding. A suicidal thought is not a suicidal wish. Every thought is a trial action, itself a compromise of instinctual impulse and defense. A suicidal wish is not a suicidal intention. Not every wish is intended yet for action. A suicidal intention is not a suicide attempt. Intentions are subject to further intrapsychic testing—actually, a series of tests. A suicidal attempt is not yet the act of suicide. Indecision and compromise formation continue. Even a suicidal act is not yet suicide. The intention is still not unequivocal, or its results assured. Finally, there is suicide. Even here there is not always finiteness, especially now that there is a question of when death actually occurs.

Anyone who wishes totally to die, with no ambivalence or indecision, has the means of bringing it about. No one lacks the power to do so. A gun or a jump assures death with most certainty. Gas can be stopped, a telephone off the hook can lead to help, even the gruesome head in the oven can be taken out. It is remarkable what creativity can go into leaving loopholes in otherwise most ingeniously contrived methods. No method assures an unequivocal decision. There is a joke in which a man looks out of his window in the middle of a skyscraper and sees a body hurtling downward. "How's it going?" he asks. "I don't know yet," replies the plunger. (It is strange that I heard this as occurring in San Francisco. Maybe that is because I live in Los Angeles.)

Even the jump, and probably the gun, do not eliminate the opposite wish while one is still alive. At the 50th-anniversary celebration of the Golden Gate Bridge, a rare jumper who survived the leap from the bridge described his experience: "From the instant I saw my hand leave

the railing, I knew I wanted to live. I was terrified out of my skull."
He remembered waking up swimming. "I was screaming, 'Oh, God,
save me! Oh, God, I want to live.'" When one intends the act of suicide
more completely, a news item such as the following appears: A woman,
age 27, walked into a schoolroom, went to the front of the class, said,
"I'm sorry I have to do this," pointed a gun at herself, and pulled the
trigger. It misfired. She then shot the gun at the wall, pointed it again
toward herself, and this time died before the bewildered class.

The Contribution of Decision Theory

The theoretical armature of my running formulation is based on my
concept of decision theory. Although psychoanalysis has contributed
knowledge of the complex workings of the unconscious, this has not
involved to an equal degree all aspects of unconscious mental activity.
Because of the sequence of psychoanalytic discoveries, human beings
were seen first in their reactive aspects, reacting to instinctual drives
from within, and the effects of external traumatic events from without.
During the second half of the psychoanalytic century, ego psychology
was added, but this too at first mainly in its defensive aspects. With
Hartmann (1939, 1950), Rapaport (1951, 1958), and the ego psychologists
who followed, active ego functioning was finally seen in its adaptive
and nonconflictual aspects.

Psychoanalytic decision theory, however, has always lagged behind.
Decision theory has been left to mathematicians and game theorists,
the military, logistic experts, and players and gamblers at games of
chance. But human decisions are as much about emotions as about
numbers and things. As a background to the analysis of the decision
for suicide, I utilize a description of psychoanalytic decision theory as
contributed in a series of my own publications (Rangell, 1963a, 1963b,
1969a, 1969b, 1971, 1986), developed over decades, on the subject of
unconscious choice and decision. From a background unconscious intrapsychic process—always operative in human mental life, during the
course of thought as trial action and the testing for signal anxiety, at
various points in the intrapsychic sequential chain—the ego selects
action or defense; brings about an acute affect or chronic mood; and
chooses a symptom, perversion, or act, or other discrete or complex
compromise formation, to give expression to the conflicting forces impinging upon it.

I pass over the decisions of everyday life every minute, day, and
night (in my theory, even during sleep) to come to the big one, the
monumental decision of universal interest. The decision to terminate
one's life, leading to the most violent and finite of human acts, considered

until recently the most pathological of decisions, has more recently been recognized as encompassing some exceptions. This is an aspect only beginning to receive conscious social attention. Although the broadening of humanitarian motives in recent years does indeed pose the possibility of an arguable rationale in favor of the termination of life, I consider first the greater and still pathological segment of suicide, the most malignant of clinical conditions confronted by those dedicated to the maintenance of mental "health." "Health" is in quotation marks because of never-absent subjective aspects. We do, however, aspire to objective standards and criteria as much as the "soft" human sciences are capable of achieving.

The Range of Motives for Suicide

Human behavior, as complex a final product as exists in the animate or inanimate world, can be pared down from complexity to relative simplicity, whether with respect to phenomenological observations or explanations as to origins, which can be both parsimonious and complete. Studying the subject of dreams, Freud (1900, 1916–1917), with characteristic virtuosity, followed them in all their ramifications, and performed an opposite task as well—condensing their infinite variety into an observation that dreams are built up out of a few universal basic elements. Just as a few numbers or integers or a short musical scale can be elaborated into infinite possibilities, dreams are also concerned at bottom with a few irreducible items. Freud said about dreams that the range of subjects is rather simple: the human body, parents, children, brothers and sisters, birth, death, nakedness, and sexual life. In a similar vein, the range of motivations for the extreme resort to suicide is also not wide. The moment of decision always rests on deeper states: on the relative degrees of satisfaction or frustration; on hopes and expectations of the satisfaction of instincts (loving and aggressive), or their opposite; on the possibility of ego mastery or its unlikelihood; on superego tranquility or savagery toward the ego and the self. Again, the range is not wide. A small number of crucial ratios are the determining factors.

Conscious versus Unconscious Intention: The Role of Aggression

The decision about one's birth belongs to others. The decisions in life about one's life are one's own. In the current period of our history, the decision about one's death has been added as a subject of discussion. In retrospect it has always been there, but is only now being talked about.

The decision to terminate one's life is not an accident, unknown or unpredictable, if the life be known. Human decisions span from survival to destruction. From the impulse side, aggression—more easily defined and widely accepted than death as an instinct—can be turned inward as outward. The ego, acting for the organism, can master, even conquer the external surround, or, identifying with the surround, can turn its armament and effectiveness against the very organism it represents. The superego, guiding the ego, can exert its influence for or against the self. The body cannot count automatically on the protection of its ego. The aggressive instinct may line up with the ego against the self.

Suicide, however, can be at least partly accidental. In assigning responsibility to or thinking of the individual's active role in the decision-making process, it is well to bear in mind that the events following a decision, large or small, conscious or unconscious, are not necessarily or even typically based on long-range intention. The decision does not always count on its ultimate consequences, on the continuous stream of effects that may follow. A quick marriage to satisfy a sexual need or any other impulsive urge does not necessarily intend, in a longitudinal sequence, to bring about the long miserable life that may follow. A suicidal attempt, undertaken for one or many reasons, may result in a suicide by accident. A person going to bed under the influence of drugs and alcohol does not count on the cumulative lethal effect of the combination of both, although there could have been self-destructive or self-stimulating wishes from one or both.

Not everything that follows a decision was intended by it. In addition to the gray area of intention is the factor of ego judgment. The ego, in its intrapsychic operations, may not accurately assess the long-range occurrences that may inexorably result. There have been many suicides brought about in this ambivalent and uninformed way. Perhaps a metaphoric example of how the ego can misassess the future, how judgment and calculations can be off, is the suicide of Van Gogh in 1890 in dire poverty at the age of 37. Until then, he had sold one painting in his lifetime, for $30. One of his "Sunflowers" sold almost 100 years later for $39.9 million![1] In the dramatic situations we are confronting today, the ego's choice, even if it fails in its precise intent or accomplishes its mixed intent but leaves a loophole of inefficient outcome, can be an irreversible one.

---

[1] Since this was written, his "Irises," inspired by the garden of the mental hospital in which he spent the last year of his life, sold for $53.9 million!

The area of responsibility for conscious or unconscious intention with respect to what follows is not an unlimited one. Intentions are complicated questions to assess. From how deep do they come? A young woman whose twin infant children died in a car of heatstroke while she slept with a man next door in a mechanic's shop was spared a verdict of involuntary manslaughter because of her good intentions; that is, "she did not mean to fall asleep but only to lie on the bed to rest for a few minutes." She also stated that the man she was with had agreed to listen for the children for her (*Los Angeles Times*, April 17, 1987).

The most insightful look into the psychodynamics of depression, the most frequent prelude to suicide, comes from Freud's (1917) division between mourning and melancholia. To mourn for a loss is normal and reparative, whereas melancholia, also a reaction to loss, is pathological and destructive. The latter syndrome shares dynamics with a significant percentage of suicidal conditions. In such a pathological state, which is what presents itself typically to a psychiatrist as "a suicidal patient," the ego loathes the self; that is, the mental agent or system in which emotions are felt holds the entire self or person in abysmal disregard. Aggression or hate is actually in both directions. It does not originate toward the self, or in a postulated internal death instinct, but as aggression, anger, or hate toward others, resulting from disappointment by loved ones or from failure of love. As in melancholia, where mourning is converted into psychotic depression, aggression is also turned upon the self. Nor is its original intention outward lost or always unclear. Suicide is also a threat to others, to whom the threat is often made overtly long before the act. The moment of its execution can be unconscious murder turned inward. That this is unconsciously recognized as such may be seen in survivor guilt, which can also reach the point of danger to its bearer.

Suicide as a Plea for Love

But not all suicide is anger toward others turned against the self. Pathological syndromes, particularly those that eventuate in a single dramatic act, are most liable to generalizations and cliches. The causes of suicidal impulses and even acts vary. Suicide can also be a misguided plea for love—one that, to be sure, has gone too far. In the recent rash of adolescent suicides, this is frequently one important component.

Adolescence is a time when the need for approval, love, and reassurance against the ferocity of inner impulses is at its height. Coupled with a lack of efficiency, skills, or judgment, or a lack of ability to reflect, postpone, or apply perspective, it is more an acute swell of helplessness, a crisis of hopeless expectations, than a chronic state of self-hate. There is a fragile and unstable tolerance of the self, compared to the pressures and intensity of the drives. It is the gulf between the two that constitutes the etiology, not internally directed aggression. Cultural influences have been at work toward this. More is expected of adolescents, by others and by themselves.

The suicidal act can be sudden and unexpected, as from an acute humiliation, not a chronic psychotic lowering of self-esteem. There can be an acute crisis of impotence or its revelation—literally in a failed sexual experience in one's early, immature love life, or figuratively or symbolically, displaced onto the need to demonstrate young or early success. A high school student made a suicidal attempt after he lost an election, in part because of what the loss would mean to his parents, but more because of what it meant to himself. Suicide or homicide is not uncommon at the revelation of homosexuality to one's peers.

The Role of Hope

Alongside the chronic or acute lowering of the self-regard (Bibring, 1953), or outburst of aggression against the self (Freud, 1917), the ultimate but crucial dynamic spurring the suicidal impulse to destruction of the self is the status of hope—the ego's deep, pervasive unconscious assessment of the potential for overcoming the conditions that have brought about the present internal condition of a traumatic state with no expected path of escape. The differences among anxiety, depression, and a suicidal state have to do with the status of the complex ego affect of hope. Anxiety (Freud, 1926; Rangell, 1955a, 1968), however intense and out of control, has two faces—one facing a traumatic state, and the other the possibility of avoiding or overcoming it. There are both present danger and the potential for escape; the future is uncertain, but there is a future. In depression, the trauma is here, and the hope of averting it is gone or diminished. But this is for now. There is still a time factor and a possible change. With a suicidal urge, there is no future. Hope neither is present now nor will ever appear.

A type of ego affect described by Erikson (1950)—hope, related to trust (in objects)—assumes a dominant, diagnostic, and prognostic import. It can be a thin line from an expectation of the temporary nature of traumatic helplessness to giving up that hope. The specific dynamics that propel the ego toward the dramatic action of the termination of life, while externally kaleidoscopic, can be pared down to certain features in common. If I can attempt to be even more parsimonious than Freud was about dreams, on a subject of such individual variability, the signposts on the road to suicide can be focused and converged on the status of love, hate, and hope.

This has nothing to do with what appears on the surface. The crucial affects can be easily forgotten/repressed. Klaus Barbie, at his trial in Lyon in 1987, said that he had no hatred against minorities, Jews, gypsies, or homosexuals. "I do not know the word 'hate.' . . . I had nothing to do with the Jewish question. That was the work of a special committee" (*Los Angeles Times*, May 14, 1987).

Loss of love or of one to love, as occurs in mourning, leaves aggression to dominate over libido. This leads to a hopeless distance between the ego and the ego ideal. The ego has failed the superego, leading to guilt and to the need for and the feeling of deserving punishment. Narcissism, so much maligned when excessive, is deficient or nonexistent; the self has lost the love or protection of the ego. Or, paradoxically, is it still excessive, such as in the omnipotence in Tom Sawyer's (Twain, 1875/1958) fantasy of returning and enjoying his own funeral? "Disturbed" patients, as suicides are considered to be, are thought of as highly narcissistic. Suicide in this respect is akin to delusions, which, as in the case of Schreber (Freud, 1911), similarly stem from omnipotence, megalomania, or a feeling of influencing and being influenced by the world.

Suicide as a Path to Glory

There can also be an opposite path to the same tragic result. There is even at times something attractive, heroic, or positive about the suicidal attempt. In San Francisco, the magnetic attraction of suicide has been increased immeasurably by the beauty, nobility, and dignity of the Golden Gate Bridge, whose 50th anniversary was recently celebrated. Its strength and majesty are visualized as the background in the jumping subject's mental picture of the event. The same result can occur from other types of psychopathology besides depression, such as from manic excitement. Derring-do unto death, in a manic or hypomanic state, can be just another way to go—to defy nature, God, fate, parents, and all their surrogates. With patriotism added to the meaning of the act, along with fantasied adoration by the nation and heroic membership among the martyrs of the ages, a kamikaze pilot carries these national values to his death with the greatest pride. Or the same aristocratic tradition leads to a virtuous end by hara-kiri.

In its accompanying unconscious fantasy, the act of suicide can achieve immortality, the same result as the poets strive for, sharing in common the essence of religion. The opposite of shame is an exhibitionistic defense, a counterphobic acting out into the offending environment. The treasurer of the state of Pennsylvania (*Los Angeles Times*, Jan. 22, 1987), under indictment for criminal behavior, called a press conference, declared his innocence, pulled out a gun, placed it in his mouth, and pulled the trigger. The moment of horror appeared in photographs in newspapers across the country. The act, symbolically and in its posthumous sequelae, restored mastery over traumatic helplessness, in the only way the individual felt was possible.

Distinctions between "Suicidal" and "Suicide"

"Suicidal" is not a diagnosis but a descriptive statement of a mental state. It can be present across the nosological spectrum—from the most malignant and ominous diagnostic categories, to cognitive–affective states that some claim are the epitome of sober rationality. My only current patient who is a distinct suicidal risk is otherwise functioning exceptionally well in life. His suicidal content is a loculated area of pathology, although one that threatens his life. The suicidal act itself is a symptom, not a diagnosis, stemming from and grafted upon a developmental history that needs its own specific understanding and interpretation. Each has a current, horizontal, acute meaning, as well as a chronic longitudinal one leading up to it. As final as its effects may turn out to be, its psychological motivation is an individualistic one, not always parallel to the severity of the outcome to which it leads. I (Rangell, 1959) once showed that "conversion" should not be automatically connected with the word "hysteria," but can indicate the entire gamut of psychopathology; nor should "free" be automatically connected with the word "will" (Rangell, 1986), both of which need to be considered separately. So can a suicidal act, however finite and discrete the final outcome, be indicative of a spectrum of pre-existing factors and behavior.

There is an important distance between "suicidal" and "suicide." Whether or when one crosses it is not always easy to predict, and at times difficult to understand. The dynamics of "suicide" may be similar to, but not the same as, "suicidal." Not many patients have free-associated in depth about the dynamics of the suicidal act. A suicide note is not the same. Those patients an analyst knows in depth do not commit suicide. Those who do, the analyst does not know in depth.

One does not know the panorama before the mind in the seconds before death, by any cause. Most thoughts about what the dying person is thinking are projections of the survivor. A patient arrived in time to see his comatose father once more just before he died. He reports without any question that his father, toward whom he had lifelong ambivalence, squeezed his hands and had tears in his eyes. In a rare clinical instance, a patient on the couch associated about what went through his mind one afternoon during the Battle of the Bulge, as he crouched in a trench, with a German soldier in sight over him holding a dangling bayonet. This patient did not confirm the myth of one's entire life passing before one at such a moment of pretermination.

The state of being suicidal can be analyzed; the act of suicide cannot. One cannot analyze a dream until after it has happened, if one is to include everything up to the last precipitating stimuli. Some who commit suicide may not have been suicidal in a chronic or prolonged sense, as is the case with some who commit murder. Others have been suicidal and then commit suicide; the act then does rest on the etiological base. A profile of the subject after the fact is never the same or the equivalent of a psychodynamic depth study. I think of two patients in whom the suicidal state was turned around and averted. Were these the analyses of suicide about to happen, or only of the suicidal state? Is "suicidal" sufficiently different from "suicide"? One of these two patients was trying to calculate mathematically how many seconds it would take from jumping off a high-rise building at a certain floor until he reached the ground.

Is the analysis of a suicidal patient the averting of a suicide? Does one ever really know? A patient, during a long analysis, stated that he went through a suicidal period, which I as the analyst never thought of as such. The patient, in an acute period of combined anxiety and depression, and acute panic mixed with hopelessness and helplessness, stated that that was the closest he ever came to the actual possibility of committing suicide. I, working in my own mind on understanding the causes of the anxiety and depression and the nature of the defenses against them, and feeling sufficient confidence in the patient's ego strength, adaptive capacities, and ultimate hold on reality, did not feel a suicidal state to be a real danger, and did not respond with medication, extra hours, or the sense of an emergency. The patient always chided me after that for not caring, or for not being able to do anything about it. Was this an experience of the treatment of a suicide successfully averted, or a more typical regression during treatment? Was it a correct assessment, properly treated with a good outcome, in spite of the patient's negative residual feelings, or a therapeutic lapse (or error) that the patient himself rescued from disaster? The patient said that he could have committed suicide, that I did not care, and that I could do nothing to help him anyway. He had better not trust me in case of such a crisis occurring again.

We must be suspicious of analysts who claim many analyses of suicides, just as we must be of an analyst who claims to have analyzed 50 or 100 homosexual patients, with each analysis taking 10 years, more or less. I also hesitate to claim many such analyses on other grounds as well.

Contagion in Teenage Suicides

The rash of teenage suicides today has become an epidemiological problem of major proportions. David Hamburg (1987), the president of the Carnegie Foundation, places its social importance ahead of nuclear war as the most pressing subject of human concern. Suicide is the second leading cause of death in the 15- to 24-year age group. Of four New Jersey teenagers who died in a garage in a suicide pact, which shook middle America recently, only one had a severe and overt suicidal history. The others, although disturbed and irregular in their previous behavior, mainly "went along" (*The Record*, Northern New Jersey, 1987). The need to belong (Rangell, 1954, 1955b), operative for a decisive moment but with a fantasy of permanence, outweighed the instinct to live. Attachment behavior, a powerful antidote against separation anxiety, took precedence over the pressure of instincts whose satisfactions dwindled into an indeterminate future. The decision could have been made in a flash; it took hold temporarily but for an irreversible moment; the instinct to live was momentarily but fatally repressed.

Contagion, characteristic of hysteria, also takes hold. Four young people in the same circle of friends had died by various "accidents" in the 9 months before the group suicide. Several of them were mourning the loss of one of their leaders in a "fall" from a New Jersey palisades cliff. Three of the victims had fathers who had died by their own hands. A series of other youths identified with the event, and, as "copycats," imitated the incident, influenced by the media, fame, and other short-range but fantasied long-range goals. Two others attempted suicide in the same garage the next week. A series of "copycat" suicides and suicide attempts in the same age range appeared across the nation.

The Dynamics of Acute Onsets

Quick decisions about life and death can be made in opposite directions. Some people reflexively and automatically turn away from a mugging, or even from a murder. Others are instinctively willing to take a risk.

One's own life is not always the highest or the only priority. In a group skydiving maneuver, a woman and a man skydiver collided in midair. She was knocked unconscious. Another man jumped from the plane without opening his parachute, reached the unconscious woman diver, pulled her string first, and only then pulled his. Both survived, where 10 seconds later both would have died (*Los Angeles Times*, May 10, 1987). The dynamics of valor, of heroism or altruism, are not well known in the psychoanalytic literature.

There are writings about the organic, chemical, or structural causes or facilitators of the suicidal state or act, just as there are about depression. These include genetic and constitutional factors, and postnatal somatic and psychic structures; the latter are built upon early mother–child and other object relations, and later organic occurrences or inputs. Whatever roles, however, are played by neurotransmitters, endorphins, the neurochemistry at the synapse, the state of the limbic system, or early structural defects from postnatal and infantile experiences that have predisposed to depressive reactions, such chemical–metabolic changes as do take place during depressive and suicidal mentation are set off in life by acute or erosive cognitive–affective experiences that accompany loss, exposure to ridicule and humiliation, and fragility of the ego feeling of self.

A common mechanism behind an acute onset is sudden shame. We have seen this in recent years in events in the public domain, as a result of the power of modern technology and the news media to publicize worldwide what would heretofore have had to be faced and mastered within the confines of one's own personal social sphere at most. Robert Macfarlane's suicidal attempt early in the Iran–contra disclosures was the latest of such public happenings, occurring as the light of publicity was descending upon him. The strength of his superego was clearly visible, pitted against the morass of involvement in which he was trapped. Having studied the problems of Watergate in depth (Rangell, 1976, 1980), I could not help but be aware of the confluence of the nature of Macfarlane's dilemmas with those of his Watergate counterpart, John Dean. Both were pressed from within by a conflict of values— what we call an intrasystemic conflict of the superego, truth verses loyalty, a clash of principles. Both were confronted by the same anticipation of a sudden exposure, to the aggregate of their peers, of behavior of which they themselves did not approve.

Their decisions were not quite the same, however; the psychic outcomes or solutions were different. Dean, in a staccato delivery that many who heard it will never forget, told it all, and toppled the government. Macfarlane was also as truthful as he could be; he told the facts, but protected and praised President Reagan and Oliver North. During Dean's months of indecision, he resorted to serious alcoholism, as opposing forces within him fought for dominance and a solution. Macfarlane made a suicidal attempt. He recovered well; at one point, he told his questioners not to consider him fragile, but to fire their biggest questions at him.

Partial Suicides

There are also the common experiences and observations, in clinic and life, of what can be considered "partial suicides," in keeping with the concept of gradations: not "all or none," but the sacrifice or abandonment of a significant portion of the functional pleasures and activities of life. These are brought about in a myriad of ways, psychological and somatic: by severe restriction of object relations; by a narrowing of the criteria for sexual object choice that makes satisfaction or fulfillment unavailable; by limitation of occupational attainments; or by somatic equivalents limiting the full range of life. Examples of these last include anorexia and emaciation, or obesity, which take one out of the stream of social relations; and chronic, habitual, ego-syntonic alcoholism (one patient had blackouts every night, so that he would not have to sit up and talk to his wife, for a period of years).

Rational Suicide

Although the acute problems of adolescence constitute a social peak, the period of adolescence arrives from childhood and points to adult life. Comparable problems exerting an impact on suicidal conditions precede and outlive the adolescent years. There are also relevant developmental factors at other specific age periods in life, pathognomonic stamps of particular developmental phases. Although problems are statistically at a peak during adolescence and young adult years, there are also midlife crises and the relentless and irreversible erosions of old age. In middle life, the more mature development of skills, experiences, and resources makes for greater adaptability and capacities for sublimation, and there is less likelihood of being overtaken by critical periods or unexpected demands. A change in jobs, or even of a spouse, is not necessarily the end of one's self. There are also, however, unusual external events at any age—war, the military, a holocaust; the feeling of being overwhelmed can never be counted out. And there is always serious illness.

Problems of old age, and the question of terminal illness at any age, have brought to the fore in recent years the subject of "rational suicide"—a concept that not too long ago was regarded as internally inconsistent. The burgeoning technology that has permitted the prolongation of life (however close this may be to the mere functioning of a heart–lung machine), coupled with increasing pressures for human rights wherever these are applicable, have made this a subject of pressing and impassioned debate. Suicide today is not a proof of psychosis. Opinions have changed from when I grew up in psychiatry—from the belief that the moment of suicide was always psychotic, if psychosis was not there before, to the thought that sometimes the act is the epitome of sober rationality. The problem of rational or voluntary suicide, although it may occupy a small percentage and an atypical segment of the total suicide problem, must be worked through theoretically, as clinical and life situations become more complex.

The arguments of the Hemlock Society for voluntary euthanasia, and for "living wills" that provide permission for the removal of life support systems under certain stipulated extreme conditions, are persuasive to many, and embody high ideals and humanitarian motives. From the sympathetic play *Whose Life Is It Anyway?* (Clark, 1979), to the same libertarian considerations in support of abortion (whose body is it anyway?) or the argument in regard to involuntary commitment (whose mind is it anyway?), the argument is made to preserve the rights and freedom of the individual in an increasingly democratic and fair society. The right to end one's life, common-sense suicide, is seen as the final right—to choose a painless over a tortured, pain-racked death.

Those against the movement for secular humanism feel that this aims to legalize crimes against humanity, crimes against the whole basis of our Judeo-Christian culture. They see a correlation between increased euthanasia and "mercy" murder cases under the same banner. There were 14 occurrences nationally in 1 year of suicide in pairs, or of "mercy" killing and/or suicide of elderly couples. An elderly Florida man who shot his wife in the brain as a "mercy" killing is now serving a long jail sentence for his "crime." Others see the pressure for euthanasia as being encouraged for economic reasons, to cut down on the money needed for health care for the aged.

A patient was called upon recently to decide whether to sign permission for surgery for his comatose 95-year-old sister, who had gangrene of the leg, for which amputation was recommended. He decided not to, but to let her go. Many doctors view such decisions and actions as counter to their Hippocratic oath. Physicians are uncomfortable about being forced to do what they morally object to, to take actions they consider unethical, to be executioners rather than to sustain life. These feelings are pitted against the rights of patients or families to halt life-sustaining care—the right to death, if they so choose, for the irreversibly ill. The solution is often to leave the decision and even the act to the patient's spouse or children, with no advice or even opinion provided by the physician. With increased technical progress, new medical questions arise spanning life from birth to death, with subtle moral and legal implications yet to be solved. From who are the parents in a surrogate birth (whose child is it anyway? whose womb? whose ovum? whose semen? there are now so many variations and unknowns) to agonizing dilemmas about the termination of life, the human and ethical dilemmas confronted are bewildering and often tragic.

Suicide as a Defense against Castration

Although the decision for suicide appears on the surface to be the most pathological decision in life, or at least the most negatively motivated, we should consider and keep in reserve what I hear from a patient who, in relating his anxieties, speaks often of "a fate worse than death." Alongside the fear of death, and at times of equal valence, is the fear of survival. In an avant-garde art work by Terry Allen (1985) entitled "Grace," a tribute to the Vietnam War, the artist includes the phrase "fear of survival" as one of the most frequently experienced horrors. As far back as World War I, when traumatic neurosis was separated for the first time from the syndrome then called "shellshock," Ernst Simmel (1926)—then a young psychiatrist with the German army, who later moved to Los Angeles and lived there until his death—wrote an early paper on the war neuroses in which he stated that the fear of death in combat was a revival of and defense against castration anxiety.

This mechanism is present in less traumatic situations than combat in war. An analytic patient, reconstructing the composite experiences behind his lifelong castration anxiety, often stated that he had a feeling of "a fate worse than death." This is the feeling of the danger, which may become inescapable, of having to endure the unendurable. The pain of castration will be superimposed upon castration anxiety. The traumatic event will supersede the fear of anticipating it. The physical will combine with the mental; the total self or person will suffer; the castration trauma will radiate to annihilation of the self. To think of enduring this is worse than the concept of death. This has a developmental background as well. Infants experience fears of bodily injury, physical invasion, separation, and destruction of the self, leading up to castration focally and specifically, before any concept of the end of life (or, with it, the fear of death).

Death by one's own hand is at times a defense against the possibility of castration—castration at the hands of another, or castration by a lingering death. The process of dying is feared more than death. During the Holocaust, surviving victims have attested to incidents in which their tormentors wished to kill them slowly so they could feel and experience it more. A patient frequently associated to his horror at the concept of Jews in concentration camps digging their own graves, in order to prolong life for a few minutes, before they themselves were shot to be pushed into those same graves. He would never do that, he angrily averred, and if he had to, he would in some way or other have taken a few Nazis with him. In his own life, he considered it a triumph when he could muster up courage to speak back to a loudmouth or bully who had spoken to him harshly in an elevator or on a tennis court.

Death is not necessarily the greatest fear, nor is its avoidance the highest priority. A mother will save her child from drowning before herself. In a poll taken of Olympic athletes, they were asked whether, if a pill were available that would help them toward victory but make death likely within 5 years, they would take it; 61% responded that they would. In sentencing the Billionaire Boys Club's Joe Hunt to life in prison without the possibility of parole, a juror explained, "We decided that the death penalty was too quick. Joe Hunt needs time to sit and think about the things he did" (*Los Angeles Times*, 1987). Alongside the experience of Jonestown I alluded to in our times, we should recall that about the same number of people, 960 defenders of Masada in 70 A.D., committed suicide for a very different reason—because they preferred death to capture and slavery under the Romans.

Concluding Remarks

Thought is experimental action. Human mental life, consisting largely of unconscious fantasies, contemplates action, assesses the consequences thereof, and filters its acts accordingly. Among drive wishes entering into the compromise formations that constitute human fantasies and actions, suicidal impulses find a place in a far wider segment of thoughts than those that are called psychotic, borderline, malignant, or even pathological.

In common to this stratum of motivation is a deep unconscious will to die, however much this is kept in check and prevented from the execution of its full purpose by the strength of the opposing life instincts. The further development of this antilife force is perhaps visible in the marasmic infants studied by Spitz (1945), who, in the face of the actual absence of maternal or other external nurture, do go on to death. We may also think in these connections of the deep resistances of the id against recovery, described by Freud (1937) as operative behind interminable analyses, and reaffirmed by Stone (1973) in chronic, intractable cases.

This is to be compared with the opposite trend in the always-dichotomous human psyche, the "will to recovery" described by Nunberg (1926)—the ally of the analyst in the analytic process. The longest surviving heart transplant patient, who lived with his second heart for 18½ years, died recently in Marseilles, France, at the age of 67. Asked about his longevity as a transplant recipient, he once said, "It is perhaps because I have a passion for life, and that I have slammed the door on death. . . . I get an extra thrill out of everything I do. . . . I am the happiest man in the world. . . . That's how I live with my old chassis and my Formula One motor" (*Los Angeles Times*, 1987). This force opposes death, and suicide.

References

Allen, T. "Grace." From "Youth in Asia" series, 1985, mixed media.
Bibring, E. The mechanism of depression. In Phyllis Greenacre (ed), *Affective Disorders. Psychoanalytic Contributions to Their Study*. New York: International Universities Press, 1953, 13–48.
Clark, B. *Whose Life Is It Anyway?* New York: Dodd, Mead, 1979.
Erikson, E. H. *Childhood and Society*. New York: Norton, 1950.
Freud, S. (1900-01). The interpretation of dreams. Parts I & II. *Standard Edition, 4 & 5.*
Freud, S. (1911). Psychoanalytic notes on an autobiographical account of a case of paranoia (dementia paranoides). *Standard Edition, 12.*
Freud, S. (1916-1917). Introductory lectures on psychoanalysis (Parts I and II). *Standard Edition, 15.*
Freud, S. (1917). Mourning and melancholia. *Standard Edition, 14.*
Freud, S. (1926). Inhibitions, symptoms and anxiety. *Standard Edition, 20.*
Freud, S. (1937). Analysis terminable and interminable. *Standard Edition, 23.*
Hamburg, D. Quoted in the *Los Angeles Times*. April 17, 1987.
Hartmann, H. (1939). *Ego Psychology and the Problem of Adaptation*. (Trans., David Rapaport.) New York: International Universities Press, 1958.
Hartmann, H. Comments on the psychoanalytic theory of the ego. *Psychoanalytic Study of the Child*, 1950, 5, 74–96.
Los Angeles Times (1987). January-May.
Milgram, S. *Obedience to Authority*. New York: Harper & Row, 1975.
Nunberg, H. (1926). The will to recovery. In *Practice and Theory of Psychoanalysis, 1*, 75–88. New York: International Universities Press, 1948.
Rangell, L. The psychology of poise, with a special elaboration on the psychic significance

Allen, T. "Grace." From "Youth in Asia" series, 1985, mixed media.
Bibring, E. The mechanism of depression. In Phyllis Greenacre (ed), *Affective Disorders. Psychoanalytic Contributions to Their Study*. New York: International Universities Press, 1953, 13–48.
Clark, B. *Whose Life Is It Anyway?* New York: Dodd, Mead, 1979.
Erikson, E. H. *Childhood and Society*. New York: Norton, 1950.
Freud, S. (1900-01). The interpretation of dreams. Parts I & II. *Standard Edition, 4 & 5.*
Freud, S. (1911). Psychoanalytic notes on an autobiographical account of a case of paranoia (dementia paranoides). *Standard Edition, 12.*
Freud, S. (1916-1917). Introductory lectures on psychoanalysis (Parts I and II). *Standard Edition, 15.*
Freud, S. (1917). Mourning and melancholia. *Standard Edition, 14.*
Freud, S. (1926). Inhibitions, symptoms and anxiety. *Standard Edition, 20.*
Freud, S. (1937). Analysis terminable and interminable. *Standard Edition, 23.*
Hamburg, D. Quoted in the *Los Angeles Times*. April 17, 1987.
Hartmann, H. (1939). *Ego Psychology and the Problem of Adaptation*. (Trans., David Rapaport.) New York: International Universities Press, 1958.
Hartmann, H. Comments on the psychoanalytic theory of the ego. *Psychoanalytic Study of the Child*, 1950, 5, 74–96.
Los Angeles Times (1987). January-May.
Milgram, S. *Obedience to Authority*. New York: Harper & Row, 1975.
Nunberg, H. (1926). The will to recovery. In *Practice and Theory of Psychoanalysis, 1*, 75–88. New York: International Universities Press, 1948.
Rangell, L. The psychology of poise, with a special elaboration on the psychic significance

of the snout or perioral region. *International Journal of Psycho-Analysis*, 1954, *35*, 313–332.

Rangell, L. On the psychoanalytic theory of anxiety: A statement of a unitary theory. *Journal of the American Psychoanalytic Association*, 1955a, *3*, 389–414.

Rangell, L. The quest for ground in human motivation. Address to the first Western Divisional Meeting of the American Psychiatric Association and the West Coast Psychoanalytic Societies, October 1955(b).

Rangell, L. The nature of conversion. *Journal of the American Psychoanalytic Association*, 1959, *7*, 632–662.

Rangell, L. The scope of intrapsychic conflict. Microscopic and macroscopic considerations. *Psychoanalytic Study of the Child*, 1963a, *18*, 75–102.

Rangell, L. Structural problems in intrapsychic conflict. *Psychoanalytic Study of the Child*, 1963b, *18*, 103–138.

Rangell, L. A further attempt to resolve the "problem of anxiety." *Journal of the American Psychoanalytic Association*, 1968, *16*, 371–404.

Rangell, L. The intrapsychic process and its analysis: A recent line of thought and its current implications. *International Journal of Psycho-Analysis*, 1969a, *50*, 65–77.

Rangell, L. Choice-conflict and the decision-making function of the ego. A psychoanalytic contribution to decision theory. *International Journal of Psycho-Analysis*, 1969b, *50*, 599–602.

Rangell, L. The decision-making process. A contribution from psychoanalysis. *Psychoanalytic Study of the Child*, 1971, *26*, 425–452.

Rangell, L. Lessons from Watergate. A derivative for psychoanalysis. *Psychoanalytic Quarterly*, 1976, *45*, 37–61.

Rangell, L. *The Mind of Watergate*. New York: Norton, 1980.

Rangell, L. The executive functions of the ego. An extension of the concept of ego autonomy. *Psychoanalytic Study of the Child*, 1986, *41*, 1–37.

Rapaport, D. The autonomy of the ego. *Bulletin of the Menninger Clinic*, 1951, *15*, 113–123.

Rapaport, D. The theory of ego autonomy: A generalization. *Bulletin of the Menninger Clinic*, 1958, *22*, 13–35.

Simmel, E. War neuroses. In S. Lorand (Ed.), *Psychoanalysis Today*. New York: International Universities Press, 1944, 227–248.

Spitz, R. A. Hospitalism. *Psychoanalytic Study of the Child*, 1945, *1*, 53–74.

Stone, L. On resistance to the psychoanalytic process: some thoughts on its nature and motivations. *Psychoanalysis & Contemporary Science*, 1973, 2, 42–73.

The Record (1987). Northern New Jersey. March.

Twain, M. (1875). *Tom Sawyer*. New York: Dodd, Mead, 1958.

CHAPTER 5

Suicide Danger: Clinical Estimation and Decision

John T. Maltsberger, MD
Harvard Medical School

The clinician who is faced with the necessity of deciding how much at risk for suicide an individual patient may be is in a quandary. Diagnostic considerations, epidemiological information, a knowledge of common clinical predictors, and even the biological information that is now becoming available are all alerting and helpful, but they are not enough. Even when all such considerations are combined they often will not answer the question: "Is this patient, sitting here with me now, about to commit suicide?" Psychological tests and the increasingly sophisticated suicide rating scales are further clinical aids, but they are still not enough.

The quandary is not resolved by reliance on two common methods often employed for assessing suicide danger: the mental status examination and the examiner's intuition about the patient at hand. Relying on these two approaches gives rise to many preventable suicides, yet in common practice critical decisions about suicide danger are often based on little else.

The common-sense approach, basing assessment primarily on the mental state examination, does not allow for full consideration of several essential factors that influence the danger of suicide, and it leaves out others altogether. Many patients who commit suicide are plainly very depressed, but many others are not. Patients commit suicide when they are not depressed, when they are angry, when they are drunk, when they are delirious, when they are in paranoid panics, and even when they seem to be recovered from the distress that brought them to psychiatric attention in the first place.

This is not to say that the mental state examination does not have an essential part to play in the assessment of suicide risk; it assuredly does. The mental state examination usually allows direct assessment of the degree of the patient's despair, but not always. It will give us

Suicide and Life-Threatening Behavior, Vol. 18(1), Spring 1988 the vital if sometimes subtle clues that the patient may harbor a secret psychosis—this through minor concretisms, clang associations, or other indications of formal thought disorder. But alone it is not enough. One may say that in psychiatry and in psychological practice, the mental state examination is analogous to the physical examination. But what physician would base diagnosis and plan treatment on the physical examination alone? Only a poor one. Good doctors attend to the clinical history as well as to physical signs.

So-called "empathic judgment," when taken alone, is a poor method for deciding suicide risk. Many schizophrenic patients do not give clues to arouse our empathic alarm. Yet these patients comprise more than 70% of those who commit suicide on inpatient units. They take us by surprise when they do it, very often because their intent is not suggested to us by mental state or our personal "hunches." Clinical intuition is easily influenced by preconscious and unconscious forces, especially at times when the examiner is under stress. In deciding by intuition whether a troublesome patient needs to be admitted to or discharged from the hospital, aversive countertransference responses outside immediate awareness can color what we feel and spoil our judgment.

The Formulation of Suicide Risk

What is sometimes called the "formulation of suicide risk" offers the clinician a disciplined method for assessing suicide danger that integrates and balances the presenting clinical material from the patient's past history, his present illness, and the present mental state examination. There are five components in case formulation: (1) assessing the patient's past responses to stress, especially losses; (2) assessing the patient's vulnerability to three life-threatening affects—aloneness, self-contempt, and murderous rage; (3) determining the nature and availability of exterior sustaining resources; (4) assessing the emergence and emotional importance of death fantasies; and (5) assessing the patient's capacity for reality testing. These are now examined in more detail.

Assessment of Past Responses to Stress

The patient's past responses to stress can be weighed by a study of his or her past history, with particular attention paid to such moments of challenge as going off to school; adolescent development; disappointments in love, work, or academic life; family strains; deaths of relatives, friends, children, or pets; divorce; and such other hurts and losses as may be discovered. Here the examiner tries to get a grip on what Edwin Shneidman (1985) calls the 10th commonality of suicide—the consistency of lifelong coping patterns. We assume that patients will tend to cope in the future as they have coped in the past. It is not unreasonable to expect that a man who responded to the death of his mother 10 years ago with a depression from which he recovered after some psychotherapy can probably survive the death of a beloved child without becoming suicidal if the positive resources in his psychological field remain unchanged. But if at his mother's death the patient withdrew from others, overdosed, developed an alcohol problem, or manifested a psychosis, there may be trouble in store. Of special interest in assessing coping patterns will be any history of previous suicide attempts, their nature, purposes, and gravity. In addition, the examiner will want to know on whom or on what the patient has relied to keep going in troubled times. The examiner will also want to know whether the patient has been vulnerable to depression in the past, and whether he or she has been prone to abandon hope in the face of trouble—in other words, whether the patient is despair-vulnerable. Despair is much more highly correlated with suicide and serious suicide attempts than is depression.

The study of the life histories of suicide-vulnerable patients shows that they do not reach adulthood with adequately developed capacities to regulate themselves emotionally. Despair-vulnerability is a case in point. What is the difference between the patient who responds to some staggering misfortune with grief and mourning, but never surrendering hope, and another who falls into suicidal despondency when fate gives him some lesser knock? Granted that there may be biochemical differences between those who hope and those who despair, are these differing biochemical dispositions genetic only? An argument can be made that biochemical vulnerability to despair may be at least partly determined by the vicissitudes of personality development in childhood and later. Future research may illuminate neurochemical differences between well-mothered and ill-mothered children. We do not know what neurochemical patterns are laid down in response to early abandonment, physical abuse, unempathic responses to separation panic, repeated humiliations, and scoldings in children.

Children who are genetically and/or emotionally disadvantaged do not build up in themselves a variety of self-regulatory functions necessary for autonomous adult survival. Some of these essential functions, the want of which disposes an individual to suicide, are as follows: the ability to feel real as a separate and discrete person; the ability to moderate anxiety so that it does not crescendo into panic; the ability to feel worthwhile; the ability to control and moderate rage; and the ability to tell the difference between what one wishes or fears and what reality affords—that is, the capacity for reality testing.

Assessment of Vulnerability to Life-Threatening Affects

Shneidman (1985) writes that the third commonality of suicide, its central stimulus, is intolerable psychic pain. Patients who reach maturity with serious self-regulatory deficits are at risk of being overwhelmed with emotional agony unless there is some outside intervention.

The first variety of potentially lethal pain is aloneness, the subjective correlate of utter emotional abandonment. Aloneness is different from lonesomeness; lonesomeness is an experience softened with hope, experienced as limited in time, eased by memories of love and closeness, and attentuated with the expectation of closeness to come again. Aloneness is, in its most extreme form, an experience beyond hope. In the grips of a full flood of aloneness, the patient feels that there has never been love, that there will never be love, and that he or she is dying. This anxiety is the anxiety of annihilation—panic and terror. People will do anything to escape from this experience. The frantic patient in an agitated depression who plucks at the clothes of passers-by, begging for relief, experiences something of aloneness. Edvard Munch's famous picture "The Scream" evokes a slight echo of aloneness in many of us.

The second variety of psychic pain is self-contempt. Self-contempt in the patient close to suicide is different not only quantitatively from ordinary anger at oneself, but qualitatively as well. To be sure, the patient may be deeply and scornfully self-contemptuous. The subjective experience is not only uncomfortable; it burns. Qualitatively it is likely to be different also, because these patients feel subjectively separate from their hating consciences. One patient said he felt that he was trapped in his body at the mercy of a torturer.

Distinct from self-hate but akin to it is the incapacity for self-appreciation. Those with this incapacity feel worthless, valueless, unlovable. It is easier for people to bear the heat of a burning conscience if they feel they have some merit, in spite of all. Those who feel valueless have much greater difficulty standing up against an interior attack because they do not believe they are worth saving.

The third variety of dangerous psychic pain is murderous rage. Patients may bear ordinary anger, but when murderous hate holds sway, the patients are in danger of turning it against themselves, sometimes because their consciences will not tolerate such a feeling without passing a death sentence, but occasionally in order to protect the lives of other people. Such patients feel their control weakening; fearing they can no longer restrain themselves from murder, they commit suicide instead.

Assessment of Exterior Sustaining Resources

It is only by relying on exterior sustaining resources that those vulnerable to suicide can protect themselves from flooding by the deadly affects. Unable to regulate themselves without relying on someone or something outside the core of the self, such patients nevertheless may remain in good equilibrium as long as the necessary resource is consistently and dependably available. It is the loss of the stabilizing exterior resource that is likely to precipitate an affective flood and invite suicide. The past history will commonly give good indications of what kind of resource the individual patient must have in order to maintain emotional homeostasis. Here we turn to Shneidman's (1985) fourth commonality: the stressor, or frustrated psychological needs.

There are three classes of exterior sustaining resources on which patients depend to keep in balance—others, work, and special self-aspects. Most commonly, suicide-vulnerable people depend on others to feel real, to feel separate, to keep reasonably calm, and to feel reasonably valuable. The loss or threatened loss of such a sustaining other can lead to an explosion of aloneness, murderous fury, and self-contempt. Suicide is often triggered by the loss of a parent, a husband, or a wife. Sometimes suicide is precipitated by the death of a beloved pet. I know of one patient who has warded off suicide all her life by the companionship of a series of cats; she insists that all these cats, by now six or seven of them, are really the same original cat of her childhood. They may look slightly different on the outside, but inside each successive cat the spirit of the original lives on. This cat, by continuous transmigration of its soul, remains constant, always loving her, soothing her, valuing her, and keeping her in balance.

Sometimes patients do not depend on others for maintaining equilibrium, but on work instead. I recall one emotionally isolated child from a distant, cold family. Early in his school years he developed a passion for learning. He was an extraordinarily gifted boy and rapidly progressed through elementary grades, high school, university, and graduate study with highest honors. His personal life was always a shambles; others mattered little to him except as conveniences for the meeting of physical needs. His wife said she felt like a ham sandwich. But academically this boy, by now an eminent professor, was a great man. Learning and now teaching were everything to him. It was not surprising that his retirement precipitated a suicide crisis—a crisis that was resolved only when space was made in a colleague's laboratory for some continuing research, and provision was made for the teaching of a seminar.

A third class of sustaining resources is comprised of valued self-aspects. Some part or function of the patient's own body is commonly such a self-aspect; the patient experiences it as not being quite connected to the rest of his devaluated self. One patient, a socially isolated accountant, paranoid and chronically suicidal, was able to live on only because of his passion for jogging. At the end of his daily run he would shower and then stand before a full-length mirror, lost in admiration of what he beheld there—a fine athletic body, the final destruction of which was unthinkable. We may refer to this patient's body as an exterior sustaining resource, because emotionally what he saw in the mirror was not experienced as a part of his central self. Neither did he experience it as quite belonging to the outside. It was for him a transitional object, and a life-sustaining one.

In this aspect of case formulation, it is important not only to identify which of the necessary sustaining resources has failed or threatens to fail, but to assess as well whether or not some important person may not actually wish the patient to be dead. Often enough after suicide has taken place, we will find evidence that a relative has ignored suicide threats or otherwise complied in a patient's death through inaction.

The identification of who or what the patient must have in order to carry on, and the determination of whether that resource is available, threatened, temporarily unavailable, or hopelessly lost, are crucial steps in the formulation of suicide risk. It is the availability of exterior resources that protects the patient from despair. But equally important is the question of whether or not the patient can appreciate, take hold of, and use resources to keep alive. Some patients may be so overwhelmed with pain that they abandon their attachments in the real world and can only think of taking flight. Helping hands may be held out, but the helping hands may not be grasped.

Assessment of Death Fantasies

Assessment of the emergence and emotional importance of death fantasies is the fourth part of formulation in suicide. Though some would disagree, it is my own belief that, at least to the unconscious, there is no cessation in death. Shneidman (1985) lists the act of egression as the eighth commonality, but it seems to me that when patients speak of "putting an end to it all," they are really wishing for something like a deep sleep, a sleep of peace. Sleep is not death, but for millennia people have tended to equate the two. To the unconscious, the egression of death often amounts to an emigration to another land where things will be better. Does not the word "egression" connote a going somewhere? Going out? We may ask, going out to where?

Fantasies of going somewhere, joining somebody, in another life beyond the grave need to be asked for, explored, and assessed. When fantasies of this nature are in fact delusional, or operate with delusional force, the patient may be in danger of suicide. In situations of intense distress, illusions may be so overvalued that they operate with the intensity of delusions. The following case illustrates this point.

Mr. G, a 63-year-old retired office worker, was transferred to a psychiatric inpatient unit after surviving an almost lethal overdose of digitalis. A former alcoholic, the patient had overcome his difficulties and become widely known for his volunteer work. A stroke left him with a thalamic infarction. He experienced great difficulty in urinating. Frequent catheterization became necessary, and his leg brace was commonly wet with urine. The stroke also left him subject to severe attacks of pain in which his hand, arm, and leg felt as though they were being crushed in a vise or pierced with sharp needles—the worst experiences of pain in his entire life. Furthermore, his ailments forced him out of the home he had shared for some years with friends. What he ostensibly found intolerable were physical decay and the suffering for which he could find no relief. He had hoarded digitalis, planning to commit suicide for months, promising himself "escape" when the suffering became too much. But careful examination showed that in fact what made life intolerable was the loss of his pet dog, Fidel.

When asked what he had imagined it would be like to be dead, Mr. G began to cry, and confided that he had hoped Fidel would be there "on the other side" waiting for him. He was careful to point out he had no sense of certainty, but a strong hope, about life beyond the grave. The patient told the examiner about Fidel eagerly, in great detail, weeping all the while as he explained how inseparable they had been. Fidel had accompanied him to banquets, had appeared on the platform with him, had attracted the notice of celebrities. For years, Mr. G had secretly smuggled Fidel into movies. The dog's intelligence had been noted by everyone; the patient and his pet had enjoyed a complete mutual capacity to understand each others' thoughts and feelings. They were the closest of friends.

When Fidel was 13 years old, he developed diabetes and required insulin injections; urinary incontinence followed. On the advice of the veterinarian, the dog was given "euthanasia." After cremation, his ashes were dispersed on a beach where "by coincidence" those of a friend's wife had been scattered before. Mr. G liked to imagine Fidel frisking along beside her, keeping her company. Before this hospital admission, the patient had not seen the connection between Fidel's illness and "euthanasia" and his own incontinence and suicide attempt.

Mr. G's mother had been physically and emotionally abusive; he had relied on his father and brother to raise him. From the age of 14, he was never without a dog, and before that he would leave for school a half hour early in order to "have conversations with four dogs who lived in the neighborhood." When asked if he would have attempted suicide had Fidel remained at his side, Mr. G exclaimed indignantly, "What? Leave Fidel? Never!"

Assessment of Capacity for Reality Testing

Assessment of the patient's capacity for reality testing is the final aspect of the formulation of suicide danger. The foregoing example shows that in a patient caught up in despair—in this instance, the despair of aloneness—fantasies about a better life after death may operate with perilous intensity. It is important not only to inquire about such fantasies or beliefs, but to decide how much psychological distance the patient can place between them and himself.

Patients in profoundly depressed states may not be able to form realistic appraisals of how much they are loved and valued by others. One must ask not only whether the external sustaining resources are available, but whether the patient is able to understand and grasp that fact.

Paranoid patients may also suffer from such disturbances of reality testing that they have grown convinced others who love them are in fact dangerous traitors who want to do them ill, so that correct appreciation of the availability of others is impossible.

Conclusion

The formulative approach to assessing suicide risk that I have outlined here (see Maltsberger, 1986, for a fuller development of it) affords a disciplined method for weighing the various vulnerabilities and strengths of patients who threaten to destroy themselves, and a means of assessing and integrating the influences, both interior and exterior, that hold such patients back from or drive them toward self-destruction.

References

Buie, D. H., & Adler, G. Definitive treatment of the borderline patient. *International Journal of Psychoanalysis and Psychotherapy*, 1982, *9*, 51–87.
Maltsberger, J. T. *Suicide risk: The formulation of clinical judgement*. New York: New York University Press, 1986.
Shneidman, E. S. *Definition of suicide*. New York: Wiley, 1985.

CHAPTER 6

Suicidal Tendencies in the Elderly

Kalle Achté, MD
University of Helsinki

According to official data (Central Statistical Office of Finland, 1981), there were altogether 3,604 deaths from suicide in Finland during the years 1978–1980, and 80% of all suicides were committed by men. In 1980, the highest suicide rates per 100,000 members of the population were recorded among men aged 65–74 years (62.1), as well as among women of the same age group (22.8). In Finland, 12% of the population are over 65 years of age, and this age group accounted for 15.1% of all the suicides committed in the years 1978–1980. Suicides occur somewhat more frequently among elderly than among younger women. In one study (Achté & Lönnqvist, 1983), it was found that, in cases in which a psychiatric consultation took place at the University Central Hospital in Helsinki following an attempted suicide, 1.8% of the patients in question were over 65. The proportion of elderly people among those attempting suicide varied from 1.1% to 2.3% per year. The proportion of those who attempted suicide varied from 1.1% to 2.3% per year. The proportion of those who attempted suicide in relation to the proportion who actually committed suicide was thus lower among elderly persons.

In other words, although the frequency of attempted suicide decreases as people get older, at the same time the number of successful suicides increases. Elderly people are in fact more likely to succeed in taking their own lives than persons belonging to younger age groups. It also emerged that, whereas only 34% of unsuccessful suicide candidates under the age of 25 really wished to die, this genuine death wish was present in 76% of the over-65-year-olds (Achté, 1986). This finding suggests that elderly suicide candidates are not simply recklessly risking their lives, but in many cases have given long and serious thought to the matter. Hence, when an elderly person makes an attempt at suicide, he or she usually has a profound death wish, and therefore selects ways and means that are indeed likely to result in the fulfillment of that wish.

Elderly people accordingly tend to choose somewhat more aggressive and effective procedures for taking their lives than do younger suicide candidates. Weiss (1968) has reported that shooting is the most common method of committing suicide among American men, although hanging is more frequent in the case of men aged over 65. Poisoning becomes less common with increasing age, among both men and women. Hanging is the method of suicide most frequently selected by elderly American women. The "average" unsuccessful suicide candidate is a young woman who attempts to end her life with an overdose of medicines, with gas, or with a knife. As a rule, her motive arises from problems at home or in the family, or from difficulties in her love life. The successful suicide candidate, by contrast, is often a man who has passed middle age and who either shoots or hangs himself. Here, the motive for the deed is often concern about deteriorating health. In many such cases, depression plays a central role.

It has been established that the degree to which a person runs the risk of suicide throughout the course of his or her life is related to the level of the birth rate in the year in which he or she was born. Individuals born in years marked by a high birth rate face lifelong exposure to correspondingly stronger competition (e.g., for educational and vocational training facilities, jobs, kindergartens for their children, economic privileges, etc.). Moreover, when persons born in "prolific" years reach retirement, they are more subject to social, economic, and psychological strains. Given the fact that the proportion of elderly people in the population is steadily increasing and that aging in itself has been shown to entail a greater risk of suicide, there is now every reason to expect rising suicide rates among the elderly. Haas and Hendin (1983) have estimated that by the year 2000 annual suicide rates in elderly members of the population will have increased by 50% as compared with the current figures, provided that population forecasts are correct and that present trends of development persist unchanged.

Susceptibility to suicide increases with age and reaches its peak between the 50th and 70th years of life. Suicides and attempts at suicide on the part of women have become more frequent in recent years; this is partly attributable to the greater freedom that women are now enjoying, thanks to female emancipation, but it is also due in part to the fact that in relation to men more and more women are now living on their own. Suicide mortality rates are never a national constant, but are subject to major periodical fluctuations. Many western European countries have seen notable rises in suicide mortality rates over the last 15 years. Changes in suicide mortality rates are often linked to current environmental factors, to changes in the age structure of the population, or to differences between birth cohorts.

Environmental factors affecting suicide mortality include changes in social structure—manifested, for example, in migration, in increased competition both in education and at work, and in alterations in social work and health care. These structural changes are reflected in family relationships, in norms and attitudes, and in the content of the mass media. The impact of environmental change is often felt most strongly within certain areas and by certain groups of the population. Suicide mortality may vary significantly in these areas and among these groups, although the general situation across the country remains more or less unchanged. Because suicide rates are unevenly distributed within the population, and because suicide involves negative social factors, suicide mortality rates are considered indicative of psychosocial well-being (Lönnqvist, Louhivuori, Palonen, & Tuomaala, 1987).

The relationship between age and suicide mortality does not always remain the same. In many Western countries it has changed rapidly during the past few years. More pessimistic views hold that suicide mortality rates in a new generation are always higher than in those that have gone before, and that this tendency continues throughout the entire lifetime of a generation. Suicide mortality rates in younger age groups are therefore expected to get higher every year, and the new generation is expected to surpass earlier ones, irrespective of the age of comparison.

One point that has yet to be clarified is whether the relatively high incidence of suicide among elderly people tends to be due to loneliness and to the economic insecurity that our present-day society inflicts upon them, or whether pathological processes involving the brain specifically enhance the risk of suicide in the elderly, especially since depression is also more common in older people. Underlying suicidal acts committed by elderly individuals, it is frequently possible to discern a multifactorial etiology, compounded of loneliness, isolation, somatic illnesses, and depression. It is precisely this multifactorial pattern that distinguishes the suicidal constellation in the elderly from the motivational background of younger people attempting or committing suicide.

In a study published by Feuerlein (1977), a comparison was made between suicide patients over 65 years of age and younger suicide patients. In half of those over 65, depression was diagnosed, whereas the corresponding percentage in the case of the younger patients was 33%. In 24% of the older patients, the motive for their attempted suicide had been a conflict with the marriage partner or with another member of the family. Other factors cited as motives were either anxiety arising from a physical illness or social isolation. Economic motives were found to have been comparatively rare in this older group of patients. Among older persons who attempt or commit suicide, social isolation in itself appears to constitute a strong motivational factor. A study by Sainsbury (1955) disclosed that among persons committing suicide in London, those living alone accounted for almost 40% in the over-60 age group—a percentage considerably higher than that in the case of the younger victims.

Losses and Loneliness as a Problem of the Elderly

For many individuals, old age is a period of mounting losses. Depending on their personalities, elderly persons may well find themselves in a situation in which the social roles they have played at work, in the family, and in society and the community as a whole become progressively narrowed down; at the same time, their income, influence, status, and prestige are also diminishing. Impoverished health, illnesses, and weakening powers of perception, coupled with retardation and impaired locomotion, often add to their sense of loss. Close contacts with others come to an end when friends and relatives of their own age die or when they lose their spouses. Some old people live in a social world of steadily increasing confinement in which they lack the verbal and emotional contacts that individuals need to have with their fellow creatures. The numerous losses with which the elderly persons are confronted then often lead to isolation and severe depression. In many instances, these aging individuals experience their existence as utterly empty and pointless, and at worst they lose their motivation to remain alive.

Loneliness is the great tragedy of aging. It is intensified by the alienation of different generations from each other, as well as by the death of family members and friends. Most of the changes in the lives of the elderly have to do with loss; in fact, old age has been called "the era of losses." After every loss, an aging person has to try to pull himself or herself together and to adjust in order to be able to retain psychological equilibrium. Each loss undermines the whole that had been formed by the surviving person and other people. The reference group into which the aging person has reflected his or her identity throughout life is also subject to continuous change. Even though old persons' losses should by no means be underestimated, it must be remembered that human beings are faced with irreversible losses in every stage of life. The difference is that old persons have had many experiences of loss that they have already mourned. This, on the one hand, represents a great psychological resource, but on the other there is also the possibility that mourning has been incomplete in some area of life.

In our society, old people are particularly vulnerable to the problem of loneliness. For many old people, loneliness is a highly painful issue, as they may find it difficult to do anything to prevent or alleviate the problem. Retirement as such may already have led to experiences of loss, in the form of a decrease in the number of relationships with other people and the narrowing of a person's field of activities. It is not easy to find company for hobbies or other activities. This may often result in depression and loss of initiative. Even normal processes of aging, such as impaired mobility and hearing, may restrict a person's ability to engage in conversation with others, while the many illnesses of old age often lead to a reduction of the old person's social circle.

An old person's loneliness depends to a great extent on how the members of his or her family view the situation and whether they are willing to take responsibility for it. The degree and effects of an elderly person's loneliness are also partly determined by his or her own personality. The most serious problems of loneliness are found when the mourning of losses earlier in life has been incomplete and the person has developed an antagonistic attitude toward other people. Old persons of this kind are typically not alone in the physical sense; they are surrounded by family members, neighbors, acquaintances, and various professional groups. They are lonely because they either deny the value and existence of the people around them or do not accept their efforts to keep in touch. Another cause of loneliness may be that aging persons may be so self-absorbed that they are not interested in what others do and say, and only keep up conversation about topics that others consider boring or self-centered.

The experience of aging and the psychosocial changes associated with it, including loneliness, are usually determined by the maturity of the personality and its ability to resolve the crises associated with this stage of life. Loneliness may be easier to cope with if an aged person knows that he or she can contact a relative or a friend at any time. In the absence of other alternatives, the help provided by various "friendship services" is indispensable to the aging. Even an initially unfamiliar person who visits the old person regularly creates a feeling of safety and helps maintain contact with the rest of the community. In addition to a personal relationship, the proverbial "friend in need" may also help the lonely old person to meet other people—for example, by helping him or her to move from one place to another. A voluntary friend of this kind—whose function in work for the elderly is highly important—may be the old person's only contact. If there is no possibility of communication with other people, loneliness can become extremely distressing for the old person.

Injuries to Self-esteem in Old Age

Persons of old age suffering from injuries to self-esteem are characterized by a common problem—the problem in regulation of self-appreciation. A person with defective self-esteem is characterized by energetic impoverishment and the occurrence of various inhibitions. This may be manifested as an inability to create and maintain significant human relationships. One's work is often hampered with serious inhibitions. In more advanced age, many persons suffering from injured self-esteem are often distinguished by a feeling of emptiness and uselessness. This involves one kind of an "empty depression," including a collapse of one's own expectations towards oneself. When self-esteem is injured, there always lurks a possibility of suicide risk. The narrowing process in the presuicidal syndrome is a typical feature in injured self-esteem. Disappointments and a tendency to regressive thinking narrow down and shrink one's human relationships and one's ability to form object relationships.

People with defective self-esteem and a tendency toward suicide are often very insecure. They experience a great deal of helplessness and anxiety. They experience both consciously and unconsciously that they are threatened. In order to restore the balance of their self-esteem, they are forced more and more to deny realities and to idealize their own persons as well as their environment. If these defense mechanisms are not effective, such persons have to resort to still more primitive measures—to fantasies of a return to a harmonious primary existence. If these fantasies are replaced by action, such individuals approach a narcissistic catastrophe reaction, the fundamental purpose of which is to save self-esteem. A person with injured self-esteem who is at suicidal risk endeavors to become merged in a diffusely experienced primary object in order to gain assurance, peace, and safety. This can be death.

The changes in intellectual, psychological, psychic, and social functions that aging involves give rise to tensions against which many elderly people contrive to mobilize defense mechanisms in order to protect their own egos. This may result either in the negation or externalization of problems or in the introjection or projection of aggressiveness, which is liable in turn to provoke depression or paranoid symptoms. In some cases, an individual's self-confidence becomes so radically affected by the changes associated with aging that he or she is no longer able to endure the changed relationship to reality. Viewed from the standpoint of the narcissistic theory, suicide can thus be regarded as a "crisis of self-confidence." According to Henseler, suicide patients are weak personalities with respect to self-confidence; such persons feel threatened, anxious, and exposed. To protect their personalities, they may possibly fall back upon the negation of reality and upon idealization of their own egos. In so doing, they create fantasies centering on a "harmonious primeval state" as typically encountered in early childhood.

Aging and Body Image

Biological processes inevitably lead to aging and associated changes in body image. The situation that an aging person must face as the body changes has been compared with the growth and anxiety of adolescence. Both young persons and aging persons find that their external appearance no longer corresponds to the internal body image upon which they have based their existence. Young persons give up the body image of childhood for a new sexual body image—a strong and (from the persons' own point of view) omnipotent body. Their anxiety is partly due to the fact that they do not yet know the limits of their newly acquired power. It is this body image and the associated sense of power that aging persons give up; they become aware of the fact that their bodies are now strange, fragile, and failing. This recognition of the gradual deterioration of the body often causes an old person hopelessness and depression. Those mechanisms of defense that in adolescence worked against the anxiety caused by changes in body image are no longer adequate at the onset of old age. The only appropriate way to deal with this is to give up the desire to have a muscular, beautiful, and attractive body through a period of mourning and to integrate the onmipotent, ideal body of the past as a remembrance of bygone times, while at the same time looking after the aging body.

It is important to help aging persons find and identify the internalized experiences of their earlier physical existence and to combine them with the present body image and its functions into a new and valuable conception. Aging persons should also be given the opportunity to discuss their physical sensations with an interested listener. Talking about one's pains and sensations of pain in particular often also serves as the description of one's body and helps contain psychological anxiety. It is important to bear in mind that descriptions of pain often have a communicative aspect; they may be used to express the feeling that one's body image is being threatened and to ask for help—things that would be difficult to express in any other way. When aging persons talk abour their bodily pains, they are also constructing a new view of their bodies, which requires the help of another person.

Deteriorating health, loneliness, and retirement from employment, perhaps with a drop in income and (as is often the case) placement in a more uncomfortable environment than before, often result in psychological problems, depression, anxiety, and even delusions of a paranoid nature. According to Kral (1978), the greatest problem is the fact that old people have to adjust to the biological, psychological, and social consequences of aging in a stage of life in which their ability to adjust generally deteriorates. A certain abruptness of character is part of normal aging. This is thought to be connected with the fact that aggressive impulses, which were previously neutralized by work and an active social life, may now "get through" in the absence of an adequate number of targets. Psychotherapeutic treatment often quite decisively helps elderly presuicidal persons to orient themselves to their new bodily reality, to succeed in their grief work, and to abandon the apt functioning and strength of their youthful and adult bodies. It is very important to help elderly presuicidal persons to discover and recognize the internalized experiences of their earlier corporeality and to recombine them into a new respected concept together with their present body image and bodily functions.

Depressions of Old Presuicidal Persons

In old age, depressive disorders often manifest themselves as somatic symptoms: tiredness, fatigue, lack of energy, agitation, and fretfulness, as well as early-morning insomnia and (what is very important) danger of suicide. The change in mood is reflected in all bodily functions. A depressed presuicidal elderly person often complains of pains and aches, various disturbances of sleep, loss of appetite, and loss of weight. He or she may suffer from insomnia (or, conversely, hypersomnia) or excessive tiredness. Lack of interest and lack of enjoyment of life are typical symptoms in the presuicidal condition, as also are exhaustion, feelings of helplessness, self-accusations, and suicidal thoughts. It is not a rare occurrence in the case of the presuicidal syndrome that the depression included in it is misdiagnosed and consequently left without proper treatment. As noted above, poor health, loneliness, retirement, and so on easily contribute to causation of mental health problems, depression, and anxiety; very importantly, the presuicidal condition and thus the risk of suicide are greatly increased. The *Diagnostic and Statistical Manual of Mental Disorders*, third edition (DSM-III) lists, in the category of affective disorders, suicidal thoughts and attempted suicides as typical frequent symptoms in both depressions and dysthymic disorders (American Psychiatric Association, 1980).

Recent studies have revealed that suicide is seldom an impulsive act unheralded by any warning signs; on the contrary, as a rule it is an event that can be anticipated. Most suicide candidates voice their suicidal ideas in advance. It has been estimated that some 75% of elderly persons contemplating suicide consult their doctors only shortly before committing the act. Warning signals suggestive of impending suicide are the "cold-shouldering" and rejection of loved ones; threats of suicide, especially if they include details as to time and place; and open admission of suicidal intentions, coupled with practical preliminary measures such as setting personal affairs in order, drawing up a will, and preparing written instructions. The greatest danger of suicide is when there is a situation arising from feelings of helplessness, hopelessness, exhaustion, and failure to which the elderly person is liable to be a prey.

The factors indicative of a risk of suicide are often manifestations of very deep depression; conversely, depression involves a particularly grave danger of suicide in an elderly person. Depression in old age is common. In a depressive state, an elderly person is frightened, preoccupied with his or her physical symptoms, weary, withdrawn, retarded, apathetic, enervated, indifferent to the environment, and devoid of all drive and energy. A sense of helplessness is typical of persons who find themselves unable to control important life situations with which they are confronted. In elderly people, feelings of helplessness are often bound up with depression, and, together with feelings of hopelessness, they may well lead to suicide. Once a physician has recognized or has reason to suspect such a syndrome, it is incumbent upon him or her to help such elderly patients to realize what life can still mean, to regain hope, and to derive enjoyment from their existence. When conducting treatment, the physician should take due account of elderly patients' overall situation, their physical and mental capabilities, and the possibilities open to them. Choice of the correct antidepressive medication is also of cardinal importance.

It would be good for doctors to have sufficient time for their anxious patients. An understanding, interested, and sympathetic attitude toward a patient is most important, and without a positive doctor–patient relationship, little can be expected of the treatment. It would be beneficial for patients to be able to visit their doctors more often than normal during crises. That way, the doctors could fill in the vacuum in which patients with suicide risk often live when their circle of interests gets narrower. A wish to die often covers a fear to live. I think in most cases it is advantageous to openly discuss the problem of suicide with such patients.

An increasing volume of literature from both health and social studies suggests the need to prevent social isolation and loneliness among the elderly. A well-run senior center can protect many of its members from depression brought on by social isolation, lack of stimulus, and inferred rejection. The senior center also offers elders the opportunity to serve their peers, with the gratification and increase of self-worth that follows. Much has been written about retirement and its impact on the final years. Researchers have stressed the importance of remaining involved and in training during the later years to preserve mental health. It is unrealistic for anyone to live on for 15–25 years of retirement with nothing to do, with no purpose in getting up each day, and with no future goals.

Some Psychoanalytic Aspects

Suicide is the realization of two purposeful intentions: that of freeing oneself from evil, and that of restoring contact with an earlier almighty object of love able to liberate the individual from the evil of the inner world. Suicide is thus an attempt to purify one's inner world. In his or her mind, the patient seeks a person-to-person relationship in which both self and all decisions are surrendered to the other. Inner conflict is externalized, and the person feels victimized, the person-to-person relationship being bound to his or her concept.

Self-destruction is affected by various factors, and thus the examination of suicidal motives must include both conscious purposes and subconscious factors. Suicide is an attempt to destroy one's inner world and to solve its conflicts. The aim is often to achieve peace, to free oneself from inner evil, to reach a harmonious state by restoring an early person-to-person relationship, to surrender oneself to a persecutor, and to create images of maintaining one's self-worth. Actual death plays a minor role as a motive; it only becomes a common denominator among suicide victims when the attempt is successful (Aalberg, 1985).

Conclusions

In conclusion, the prevention of depression and suicide in old age requires a real change of attitude in society toward the elderly—a change that will guarantee every older person the right to work and to love. That was Sigmund Freud's formula for mental health, elegant in its simplicity. Erik Erikson taught that the theme of old age is the maintenance of integrity. Hemingway, who had a great fear of old age, once said, "As you get older, it is harder to have heroes, but it is sort of necessary." That insight should inspire a note of optimism for the final years (Charatan, 1984).

References

Aalberg, V. Itsemurhayrityksen motiivit. *Duodecim*, 1985, *101*, 1720–1721.

Achté, K. Suicidal tendencies in the elderly. In P. Kielholz & C. Adams (Eds.), *The elderly person as a patient.* Cologne, West Germany: Deutscher Ärzte-Verlag, 1986.

Achté, K., & Kärhä, E. Some psychodynamic aspects of the presuicidal syndrome with special reference to older persons. *Crisis*, 1986, *7*, 24–32.

Achté, K., & Lönnqvist, J. Follow-up study on the attempted suicides among the elderly in Helsinki in 1973–1979. In *Abstracts of the 12th International Congress of Suicide Prevention and Crisis Intervention, Caracas, Venezuela, October 2–5, 1983.*

American Psychiatric Association. Diagnostic and statistical manual of mental disorders (3rd ed.). Washington, D.C.: Author, 1980.

Central Statistical Office of Finland. *Causes of death in Finland 1978–1980.* Helsinki: Author, 1981–1983.

Charatan, F. B. Personal communication, 1984.

Feuerlein, W. Ursachen, Motivationen und Tendenzen von Selbst-mordhandlungen im Alter. *Aktuelle Gerontologie*, 1977, *7*, 67–74.

Haas, A. B., & Hendin, H. Suicide among older people: Projections for the future. *Suicide and Life-Threatening Behavior*, 1983, *13*, 147–154.

Henseler, H. *Narzisstische Krisen: Zur Psychodynamic des Sellostmords.* Hamburg: Rowohlt, 1974.

Kral, V. A. Neurotic reactions of the aged—their treatment. *Psychiatric Journal of the University of Ottawa*, 1978, *3*, 111–114.

Lönnqvist, J., Louhivuori, K., Palonen, K., & Tuomaala, A. Itsemurhakuolleisuus Suomessa. *Suom. Lääkäril.* 1987, *42*, 938–946.

Sainsbury, P. *Suicide in London: An ecological study.* London: Chapman & Hall, 1955.

Weiss, J. A. Suicide in the aged. In H. L. P. Resnik (Ed.), *Suicidal behaviors: Diagnosis and management.* Boston: Little, Brown, 1968.

CHAPTER 7

The Two Traditions in Suicide Research (The Dublin Lecture)

Norman Kreitman, MD, FRCP, FRCPsych
Royal Edinburgh Hospital

My great pleasure in receiving the prestigious Dublin Award of the American Association of Suicidology is enhanced by its connection with the name of Louis Dublin. His interests were those of the true polymath, and he could comment authoritatively on a great range of themes— from general sociology, anthropology, and the history of social attitudes to suicide, religion, legal provision and jurisprudence, and epidemiology. Yet even he stated in 1963 that the volume of work being generated in the field of suicide studies was already becoming almost impossible to monitor. The present deluge of writings would have rendered even a man of his immense talents almost as desperate as the rest of us who attempt to keep if not abreast of, at least in sight of, the expanding boundaries of our subject. Yet in studies of the causes of suicide, and of its distribution in society, it seems to me there are just two basic traditions, which are as active today as ever they were. These might be described, in shorthand, as the psychiatric and the sociological. To identify them with any clarity, however, it is necessary to go back a little way in the history of suicide research.

It is a most vulgar error to assume that anything written before the contemporary era can be ignored, or that our predecessors were less perceptive than we are. Nevertheless, it is convenient to adopt the fiction that the scientifc study of suicide began in the period just prior to the publication of Durkheim's book on the subject in 1897; even then, we should appreciate that Durkheim was able to draw on statistical and other reports extending back almost a century. Durkheim was

Lecture given on receipt of the Dublin Award at the joint meeting of the American Association of Suicidology and the International Association for Suicide Prevention, San Francisco, May 1987.

concerned to establish and consolidate within the field of suicide studies the new science of sociology, and needed therefore to take issue with the prevailing medical ethos of his time. The target for much of his criticism was his fellow countryman Esquirol, though the debate was somewhat one-sided in that Esquirol had been dead since 1840, over 50 years before. Moreover, with hindsight, it can be seen that the issue was clouded by the fact that each protagonist addressed rather different questions: Esquirol and his followers commented on the risks of suicide among the mentally ill, whereas Durkheim was essentially concerned with the converse issue of the proportion of mentally ill among all suicides, and also with the question of whether such data were relevant for explaining national suicide rates. He recognized that only epidemiology could resolve these dual questions, but it is interesting that he believed such studies to be intrinsically impossible. Meanwhile, he exercised himself in demolishing the arguments put forward by those with the temerity to believe that psychiatric illness had something to do with suicide.

Esquirol's own writings appear, in this instance at least, to have been somewhat robust. "Suicides are mentally alienated," he stated, but his pupils and contemporaries were rather more tentative. About 1846, Moreau de Tours wrote, "Should suicide be regarded in all cases as the results of mental alienation? Without wishing to dispose here of this difficult question, let us say generally that one is instinctively the more inclined to the affirmative the deeper the study of insanity which he has made, the greater his experience and the greater the number of insane persons whom he has examined" (p. 287).

Much time had to pass for documentation concerning the role of mental illness in an unselected series of suicides to be produced, as compared simply to follow-up studies of identified patients. There is said to have been a report by Stearns of Massachusetts in 1921 proposing that 50% of suicides suffered from mental illness, and 40 years later (note the interval) Ringel of Vienna cited a proportion of about a third. But by that time a new kind of psychiatric inquiry had emerged. It was foreshadowed by Sainsbury's (1955) classic study of suicide in London, which examined, among many other things, the documentary evidence on a series of suicides to ascertain the proportions who had ever received psychiatric care. The next advance, which in effect set the contemporary scene, was to move to direct study of the lives of suicides by questioning in detail those who knew them well, especially in the latter stages, and adapting the principles of the "psychological autopsy" pioneered by Norman Farberow and his colleagues. The St. Louis studies of 1959 are the prototype, wherein Robins, Murphy, Wilkinson, Gassner, and Kays (1959) reported that virtually all their large series of suicides were suffering from a psychiatric disorder, mostly of a classical and easily recognized form. Shortly afterwards, Dorpat and Ripley (1960) from Washington State reported on a similar project, with very similar results. From Sussex and the south of England, Barraclough, Bunch, Nelson, and Sainsbury (1974) again reported that 94% of their series had a readily diagnosable illness, and later work from Australia by Chynoweth, Tonge, and Armstrong (1980) once more came to a similar conclusion.

Various critics, including Louis Dublin (1963), have pointed to possible weaknesses in work of this kind. One has to do with the unreliability of the categorization of individuals, concerning both whether or not they are mentally ill and the specific types of illness being diagnosed. This is a weighty point. The authors I have quoted were in general using the *International Classification of Diseases*, which at that time did not have any precise operational criteria attached to it. It is true that in some of the studies diagnostic criteria were spelled out by the authors, but that does not establish their reliability or circumvent the problem of establishing comparability between one study and another. It may well be possible to clarify matters by going back to the admirably documented reports by all these writers and applying one of the modern sets of diagnostic criteria to the data. Indeed, an attempt has been made to validate the St. Louis series in just such a way (Robins, 1981). Future studies should of course take pains to try to advance diagnostic precision, and no doubt will do so.

The other problem is the tendency toward bias in the assessment of mental status, due to knowledge that individuals have indeed died by suicide. The use of more rigorous and more reliable diagnostic criteria may reduce the problem to some degree, but the most satisfactory procedure is to ascertain how commonly the deceased have been diagnosed, and by what criteria, prior to death. There is indeed a substantial body of data on this question, since documentary studies are so much easier to carry out than in-depth interviewing. The proportion typically quoted varies somewhat; our own data at the Royal Edinburgh Hospital give a figure of 52% for prior treatments, but a reasonable average value would be around 40%. This rises if consultation with primary care physicians for psychological symptoms is also counted, and becomes higher still if all forms of medical contact are enumerated, especially with respect to just the few weeks prior to death. Formal diagnosis by psychiatric service is, of course, the most robust indicator, and the data serve to buttress the reports of high levels of mental illness among suicides. The estimates so provided are, of course, lower than those reached in the "psychological autopsy" type of project, but on the other hand it is well established that treated morbidity represents only a small proportion of all those in the population who meet the criteria for psychiatric disorder. This is particularly true for affective disorder, alcohol dependence, and drug abuse—the three diagnoses that occur most commonly in reported suicides.

On balance, then, I feel that the painstaking work demonstrating the very high frequency of quite palpable psychiatric disorder in random samples of suicides is persuasive to the point of near-certainty. From a public health perspective, it appears to be the primary determinant. But let us go back again to 1897. Durkheim (1897/1951) argued at length that a psychiatric approach to suicide is inadequate, and perhaps basically misconceived. In part, he based his arguments on the intrinsic nature of "neurasthenia," on the difficulty of defining "suicidal insanity," and so on; these contentions are necessarily enmeshed in the contemporary theories of psychological abnormality and carry little impact today. But, much more cogently, he argued from current knowledge of the epidemiology of mental illness, showing that the picture did not square with the epidemiology of suicide as it was understood in his time. Had he had at his disposal the data bases that are now available, or even if he had chosen to utilize in the first few chapters of his book some of the data that he cited toward the end of the volume, he could surely have flattened the opposition. Thus, with respect to the precipitate fall in suicide rates that so regularly occurs with the onset of a war or even the threat thereof, he could have demanded (in icy tones if necessary) if it were seriously to be considered that the number of lunatics in the society drops by a third in the course of a day or so with the onset of hostilities. Or, again, if for a moment one assumes cross-national comparisons to have any validity at all, did the suicide rate for England in 1870 (which was cited at 66 per 1,000,000) when compared to that of Denmark in the same year (namely, 258 per 1,000,000) imply that the Danes went crazy at four times the rate of the English? (Hamlet thought the answer was probably no, but I will set that opinion aside for the moment.)

Whatever the details, Durkheim's general contention that variations in suicide rates can be understood in terms of social changes as they occur over time, or between nations, or within large groups, has proved immensely fertile. For all its defects, Durkheim's theory is still the most widely employed. In saying this, I am well aware of the major theoretical and empirical contributions by writers such as Henry and Short (1954) and Gibbs and Martin (1964), but for present purposes these can be viewed as extensions of the Durkheimian tradition. That tradition too has been challenged, and I want just to mention two of these points of contention.

Some time back, a criticism was launched of the legitimacy of any kind of argument based on suicide statistics (such as those Durkheim had widely employed), on the grounds that all such statistics are biased, and biased in a very special way (Douglas, 1967). Essentially, this position was an early example of what has now come to be known as "social constructivism." In this view, it is stressed that in human affairs definitions are not discovered, but are constructed; they reflect meanings. In particular, suicide statistics are derived from the judgments of coroners working in the context of elaborate social structures. What the student has available, then, is what the coroner thinks. Moreover, since coroners and those working with them will tend to be familiar with what sociologists and psychiatrists believe about suicide, they will accordingly be influenced in their own judgments when identifying suicidal deaths. A person found dead who was mentally ill and socially isolated will be categorized as a suicide largely because received wisdom suggests such a verdict *a priori*. Thus anyone who looks for confirmation of current theories among suicide records or suicide statistics will discover nothing but a self-fulfilling cycle.

This criticism created a stir that I judge is now subsiding—largely, I suspect, because it is slowly being realized that to identify a question as one involving meanings is not the same as removing the matter from the realms of empirical research. On the contrary, questions about meaning are basic to epidemiology. Most (if not quite all) of the issues raised by the contructionist critique not only can be, but long have been, widely researched by students of suicide. The upshot of this work is, I think, rather impressively in favor of the continuing usefulness of suicide data, although of course they must be sensibly treated, and we have gained useful understanding of their limitations.

More purely sociological critics have pointed to another difficulty with the Durkheimian approach, which relates to a certain circularity of arguments within his system. They point out that it is not very informative to explain the high suicide rates of, say, the divorced in terms of anomie, if anomie is in turn defined as being divorced or some similar state. There is some justice in such comments, but the implication, I take it, is the need to flesh out more fully the kinds of concepts that Durkheim sought to express, and to do so with reference to contemporary concepts more capable of being operationally defined.

It would appear, then, that Durkheim's approach is very much alive, even if a great deal remains to be done to rectify its weaknesses. But at this point I would like to touch on an important aspect of Durkheim's own writing concerning what *type* of explanation is being advanced for suicide. Ideas such as anomie were originally intended to apply to *social* groups; the other subtypes of suicide that Durkheim described, whether in pure form or as one of the many hybrids, were similarly intended to refer to social and not psychological phenomena, although it must be admitted that his writing is often unclear on this point. Certainly in practice the distinction has been either overlooked or deliberately overridden by those involved in work with suicidal individuals. It is not without a certain irony that a tradition of research that originated in protest as an exclusively individual perspective should have led to insights that are as much psychological as sociological in character.

Much more could be said about the strength and possible weaknesses of sociological and social-psychological studies as they have branched out since the beginning of this century. My point of emphasis, however, is that this line of work, and the medical or psychiatric one to which I referred earlier, have been carried forward with relatively little interaction between them. Yet to any impartial student, surely the most glaring question in the contemporary scene is precisely how the two traditions are to be understood in relation to each other. At present, there is little empirical research that even tries to bridge the gap (however, see Maris, 1981). There are of course conceptual difficulties, in that the unit of study of psychiatric epidemiology must be the individual case, while for macrosociology it is the social unit. But I do not believe that difference is insuperable, since, as I indicated earlier, something analogous to (though not identical with) a sociological formulation can be constructed in individual terms employing Durkheimian concepts. Moreover, there are already a number of observations that strongly support the usefulness of a marriage between the two research positions. We know, for example, that attempts to distinguish within the major diagnostic groups of patients those who go on to suicide and those who do not have never succeeded in clearly segregating subgroups that can be defined in clinical or symptomatic terms. On the other hand, the social environment of a patient appears to be of paramount importance as a predictor. Conversely, no study of social disintegration, migration, upward or downward social mobility, or any similar candidate group has successfully identified a collective in which the *majority* of its members proceed to suicide. It requires no great leap of imagination to suggest that it may be the psychological health or impairment of the individuals within the high-risk group, socially defined, that determines which persons live and which die tragically, by their own hands.

It is my hope that the future will bring us many projects that address just such a span of issues, and that take their interaction as their central objective. They will be expensive and time-consuming, since they will have to involve data collection at an individual level. They will require interprofessional collaboration at its best, and the necessary institutional framework to support such interaction. Yet I would argue that further monocular perseveration with either of the single main traditions is unlikely to be rewarding, and that it is time for us now to focus both eyes at once. I would like to think that Louis Dublin, who united so many diverse strands of knowledge, would have approved just such a program.

References

Barraclough, B., Bunch, J., Nelson, B., & Sainsbury, P. A hundred cases of suicide: Clinical aspects. *British Journal of Psychiatry*, 1974, *124*, 355–373.
Chynoweth, R., Tonge, J., & Armstrong, J. Suicide in Brisbane: A retrospective psychosocial study. *Australian and New Zealand Journal of Psychiatry*, 1980, *14*, 37–45.
Dorpat, T. L., & Ripley, H. S. A study of suicide in the Seattle area. *Comprehensive Psychiatry*, 1960, *1*, 349–359.
Douglas, J. *The social meanings of suicide*. Princeton, N.J.: Princeton University Press, 1967.
Dublin, L. I. *Suicide: A sociological and statistical study*. New York: Ronald Press, 1963.
Durkheim, E. *Suicide: A study in sociology* (J. Spauling & G. Simpson, Trans.) Glencoe, Ill.: Free Press, 1951. (Originally published, 1897.)
Esquirol, J. Alterations pathologiques observées chez les suicides. *Maladies Mentales*, 1838, *5*, 639.
Gibbs, J., & Martin, W. *Status integration and suicide*. Eugene: University of Oregon Press, 1964.
Henry, A., & Short, J. *Suicide and homicide*. Glencoe, Ill.: Free Press, 1954.
Maris, R. *Pathways to suicide*. Baltimore: Johns Hopkins University Press, 1981.
Moreau de Tours, A. *Annales Medico Psychologiques*, 1846, *7*, 285–290.
Robins, E. *The final months*. New York: Oxford University Press, 1954.
Robins, E., Murphy, G. E., Wilkinson, R. H., Jr., Gassner, S., & Kays, J. Some clinical considerations in the prevention of suicide based on a study of 134 successful suicides. *American Journal of Public Health*, 1959, *49*, 888–899.
Sainsbury, P. *Suicide in London* (Maudsley Monograph No. 1). London: Chapman & Hall, 1955.
Stearns, H. W. Suicide in Massachusetts. *Mental Hygiene*, 1921, *5*, 752–777.

CHAPTER 8

Conceptual, Methodological, and Sociocultural Issues in Black Youth Suicide: Implications for Assessment and Early Intervention

Jewelle Taylor Gibbs, PhD
University of California—Berkeley

Suicide among blacks is a youthful phenomenon. At a time when they should be developing an identity, exploring career options, or beginning a family, too many young blacks are destroying themselves, either by suicide, by homicide, or in fatal accidents. In all other ethnic groups except American Indians, suicide rates increase with age, yet the suicide rate among blacks peaks during the young adult years (25–34) and decreases with age. Suicide is the *third* leading cause of death in black youths in the 15–24 age group, after homicides and accidents; and 47% of all black suicides occur in the 20–34 age group (U.S. Bureau of the Census, 1986).

In the past 25 years, the overall suicide rate of black youths (aged 15–24) has more than doubled, with males between 20 and 24 accounting for most of that increase. However, while scholarly interest in the phenomenon of youth suicide has grown rapidly during this period, few researchers have focused on the particular issues involved in the suicidal behavior of black youths. Thus, a review of the literature on black youth suicide reveals limited conceptual approaches, few clinical investigations, and even fewer empirical studies of this group.

This gap in the literature is of particular concern, in view of the comparative trends in rates and patterns of suicide and suicidal behavior among black and white youths in the 15–24 age range. From 1960 to 1983, the suicide rate for black youths in the 15–24 age group doubled for black females (from 1.3 to 2.7 per 100,000) and nearly tripled for black males (from 4.1 to 11.5 per 100,000), following almost identical trends in the pattern of white male and white female suicide rates (see

TABLE 8-1.   Black and White Youth Suicide Rates per 100,000
Residents (15–24 Age Group)

Group	1960	1970	1980	1982	1983
Black females	1.3	2.8	2.3	2.2	2.7
Black males	4.1	10.5	12.3	11.0	11.5
White females	2.3	4.2	4.6	4.5	4.6
White males	8.6	13.9	21.4	21.2	20.6

Note. From U.S. DHHS (1985).

Table 8-1). Black male suicide rates in this age group were over four
times the rate for black females—a ratio that had increased since 1960.
However, a closer look at the data reveals peak rates in 1970, 1972,
and 1979 for black males, compared to peak rates for black females in
1967, 1971–1972, and 1976–1977 (U.S. Department of Health and
Human Services [DHHS], 1985).

It is important to disaggregate this data to note different patterns
and rates for the 15–19 and 20–24 age groups (see Table 8-2). First,
males and females in the 20–24 group had higher rates than those in
the 15–19 group. Second, the rates for black males aged 20–24 accounted
for most of the increase in the overall black youth suicide rate, while
the other three groups increased at a much slower rate. Third, the ratio
of male to female rates was much higher in the 20–24 age group than
in the 15–19 group (U.S. Bureau of the Census, 1986).

Finally, in spite of much propaganda to the contrary, black youth
suicide rates appear to be leveling off and are not converging on white
youth suicide rates, but have maintained a fairly predictable relationship
to white rates since 1958, with only a few exceptions (i.e., white male
rates averaged 1.8 times higher and white female rates averaged 2.5
times higher than black males and females, respectively) (see Table

TABLE 8-2.   Black Youth Suicide Rates per 100,000 Residents by Subgroups

Group	1960	1965	1970	1971	1975	1980	1982
Blacks aged 15–19							
Females	1.1	2.2	2.9	3.4	1.5	1.6	1.5
Males	2.9	5.1	4.7	5.0	6.1	5.6	6.2
Blacks aged 20–24							
Females	1.5	3.5	4.9	6.5	5.2	3.1	2.9
Males	5.8	12.3	18.7	16.1	21.1	20.0	16.0

Note. From U.S. Bureau of the Census (1986).

TABLE 8-3. Death Rates for Suicide, by Age, Race, and Sex, per 100,000 Residents:
United States, 1960–1982

Year	Black females			Black males		
	Total 15–24	15–19	20–24	Total 15–24	15–19	20–24
1982	2.2	1.5	2.9	11.0	6.2	16.0
1981	2.4	1.6	3.2	11.1	5.5	17.1
1980	2.3	1.6	3.1	12.3	5.6	20.0
1979	3.3	2.1	4.6	14.0	6.7	22.5
1978	2.7	1.3	4.1	13.0	5.5	21.9
1977	3.7	2.4	5.3	13.0	6.0	21.6
1976	3.7	2.5	5.1	13.0	7.0	20.6
1975	3.2	1.5	5.2	12.7	6.1	21.1
1974	3.4	2.5	4.5	11.1	4.9	19.1
1973	3.3	2.1	4.7	12.7	5.7	21.9
1972	4.7	3.0	6.7	14.7	8.1	23.5
1971	4.8	3.4	6.5	9.7	5.0	16.1
1970	3.8	2.9	4.9	10.5	4.7	18.7
1969	4.1	3.0	5.6	9.2	4.4	16.0
1968	2.9	1.8	4.2	7.2	3.8	12.3
1967	3.8	3.3	4.4	7.1	3.1	13.0
1966	2.3	1.9	2.9	7.8	4.3	13.0
1965	2.7	2.2	3.5	8.1	5.1	12.3
1964	1.9	1.9	2.0	7.5	3.6	12.9
1963	N.A.	N.A.	N.A.	N.A.	N.A.	N.A.
1962	N.A.	N.A.	N.A.	N.A.	N.A.	N.A.
1961	1.6	1.2	2.1	6.8	3.6	10.9
1960	1.3	1.1	1.5	4.1	2.9	5.8

Note. From Taube & Barrett (1985). N.A., not available.

8-3). They have also remained remarkably stable since 1978, with only slight annual variations among blacks in the 15–24 age group.[1]

If these suicide rates of black youths are so much lower than white rates and appear to be leveling off, why should we be concerned about the problem at all? Suicide is a significant problem for black youths not only because it is one of the leading causes of mortality in this age group, but also because it has a disproportionate impact on the black population, which is a youthful population with a median age of 25.8 years (U.S. Bureau of the Census, 1986). As the proportion of nonwhites in the total youth population is expected to increase to approximately 20% by the year 2000, at present rates the actual number of suicides will increase substantially, with negative consequences for the black

[1] Rates of black females exceeded those of white females in the 15–19 age group in 1966–1967 and 1969–1972, but have been lower ever since 1973.

community and the general economy (Ozawa, 1986).[2] Finally, a growing concern for young black women is the ratio of marriageable men available to them in the prime years of family formation and child rearing, which sociologist William Wilson has estimated as 47 employed black males for every 100 marriageable black females in the 20–24 age group. Of course, any increase in male suicide rates in this age group would further reduce the availability pool of marriageable males for young black women (Aponte, Neckerman, & Wilson, 1985). This "male marriageable pool index" ratio not only has negative implications for black family formation, but also suggests the possibility of increased stress, depression, and other suicidal risk factors for young black women.

The present chapter has four primary goals: (1) to examine methodological issues regarding suicide among black youths; (2) to evaluate three conceptual perspectives on black youth suicide; (3) to delineate sociocultural factors that contribute to differential rates of suicide between black males and females; and (4) to propose implications for assessment and strategies of early intervention addressed to black youths who are at high risk for suicidal behavior.

Methodological Issues

Reliability and Validity of Data Collection

Some social scientists and criminologists have proposed that suicidal behavior is simply one form of violent behavior that characterizes the self-destructive life styles of low-income inner-city black youths (Hendin, 1969; Seiden, 1972). Statistics indicate that the three leading causes of deaths among black males aged 15–24 are homicide, accidents, and suicide (U.S. Bureau of the Census, 1986). As noted earlier, black males in this age group have higher rates than black or white females or white males in all three of these categories, except for male suicide.

In evaluating this pattern of black youth involvement in suicide, homicide, and accidental deaths, it is important not only to note the relationship among these three types of violent deaths, but also to raise questions about the validity and reliability of the data, particularly with regard to the statistics on homicide and "unintentional" accidental deaths in this group. It has been suggested that some black males deliberately set up violent confrontations with the police in order to

---

[2] The category "nonwhite" in the census data usually is comprised of 90% or more blacks.

provoke lethal retaliatory action or "victim-precipitated homicide" (Breed, 1970; Seiden, 1972). Examples of this phenomenon are seen in the aggressive antiauthority behavior of the Black Panthers (several of whom were killed in gun battles with the police); the revolutionary rhetoric of the Symbionese Liberation Army in 1974 (whose leaders died in a fire after a gun battle with police); and the escalation of community conflict by members of MOVE in 1986 in Philadelphia (who met a similar fate). Some experts would argue that many young ghetto males subconsciously set up similar situations when they engage in gang fights, high-risk burglaries, and other explosive situations that combine the use of lethal weapons, alcohol or drugs, and confrontational behaviors. How many of these youths are consciously or unconsciously flirting with death, even inviting destruction, so that they can remove themselves from an intolerable existence without actually taking responsibility for the ultimate act of self-annihilation? Some of these apparent homicides could be classified as forms of "revolutionary" or "fatalistic" suicide, in Durkheim's (1897/1962) terms.

Another question of validity is the categorization of "unintentional" accidents. Black males have a high rate of fatal automobile accidents, 69% of which involve alcohol (U.S. DHHS, 1986). While no age breakdown was available for this data, it is also known that about three-fourths of all youth fatal accidents involve alcohol, although the rate for black youths may be lower, since black youths have lower drinking rates than white youths (U.S. DHHS, 1986). However, many of these single-car accidents, whether or not liquor is involved, may in fact be "autocides"—another way of disguising suicidal behavior, perhaps to ease the pain of surviving family members. Other forms of "accidental" deaths, such as drownings, falls from high buildings, and industrial accidents, may also be disguised suicides in this group.

Some researchers have suggested that many deaths from drug overdoses can be viewed as a form of suicide (Smart, 1980). Black youth are three times more likely to be in treatment programs for drug-abuse-related problems than whites (National Institute on Drug Abuse [NIDA], 1985), and are also more likely to report a primary problem with heroin, cocaine, and PCP, all addictive drugs with serious health consequences. Heroin, cocaine, and PCP were the three most frequent causes of drug-related deaths among black youths in 1980, with 45% of these deaths heroin-related. From 1982 to 1984 alone, cocaine-related deaths among black youth tripled, while the percentage of PCP-related deaths involving all blacks increased from 50% to 58% between 1983 and 1984 (NIDA, 1985).

There are also problems with the reliability of youth suicide statistics, including a general tendency to underreport or misreport suicides as accidental or "undetermined" deaths; state and regional variations in reporting; and cultural attitudes of family members, which often result in covering up the suicidal act (Shaffer & Fisher, 1981; Warshauer & Monk, 1978). Several authors have proposed that the true suicide rate, particularly for blacks, would be much higher if the "unqualified" suicides were combined with the category "undetermined deaths" (Shaffer & Fisher, 1981; Smith & Carter, 1986; Warshauer & Monk, 1978). This would be particularly true for black youths, many of whom come from religious families where suicide is culturally and spiritually alien and is thus viewed as an intolerable social stigma; this may partially account for much lower rates for blacks in general in the South and rural areas (Bush, 1976).

Thus, black youth suicide rates would probably be much higher, particularly among males, if intentional accidental deaths, deliberate drug overdoses, and even "victim-precipitated" homicides were included as methods of voluntary self-annihilation. Furthermore, if there were improved case finding and consistency in classification across local jurisdictions and by medical examiners or coroners, the rates of black youth suicide would be more valid and reliable (Shaffer & Fisher, 1981; Warshauer & Monk, 1978).

Case Examples

Two case examples illustrate the human tragedy behind these statistics and methodological issues, as well as the difficulty of making generalizations about black youth suicide.

Case 1. Karen: In Search of an Identity.   Karen, a recent graduate of an Ivy League college, was having considerable difficulty in deciding whether to work or return to graduate school. She found she could not communicate her self-doubts and her ambivalent feelings toward whites to her successful middle-class parents. During the summer after her college graduation, she broke up with her boyfriend, withdrew from most of her friends, and quarreled constantly with her parents. Late one summer afternoon, after a bitter argument with her father, she was driving alone on the freeway when, according to several witnesses, her car suddenly accelerated and she crashed into a bridge abutment. Karen was killed instantly on the eve of her 22nd birthday.

Case 2. Robert: No Place to Be Somebody.   Robert, abused and abandoned by his alcoholic mother as a child, had been reared in foster homes since the age of 3. By age 16, he had a police record, was failing in school, and was known as a "loner." When Robert's working-class foster parents felt they could no longer tolerate his increasingly aggressive behavior, he was transferred to a group home, where he became sullen and withdrawn. After he attacked one of the counselors for saying that no one really cared about him, Robert was sent to juvenile hall. On his third morning in detention, the attendant discovered Robert hanging in his room. He left a note on his pillow that said, "I haven't got nobody and I ain't ever going to be nothing. Tell my mom goodbye, if you ever find her."

In addition to the obvious methodological issues, these two very disparate case examples raise some significant conceptual and sociocultural questions about black youth suicide; that is, what theoretical perspectives and sociocultural factors are useful in advancing our understanding of the dimensions of suicide in this heterogeneous group?

Conceptual Perspectives on Black Youth Suicide

Three major conceptual approaches that have been used to explain suicide among black youths are the following: (1) the sociological approach; (2) the psychological approach; and (3) the ecological approach. Although it is not possible to discuss these approaches in depth here, it is important to summarize them briefly and to comment on their heuristic value in furthering our understanding of black youth suicide.

First, the sociological perspective is epitomized in the theories of Emile Durkheim (1897/1962), the 19th-century French sociologist, who proposed that there were three types of suicide, all related to the lack of fit between the individual and the society. Particularly relevant to black youths are his concepts of "anomic suicide," which increases as the social integration of individuals decreases, resulting in weaker social bonds and group norms; and "fatalistic suicide," which occurs when individuals cannot tolerate excessive social restrictions and oppressive regulations. Durkheim's classic views are reflected in the more contemporary theory of status integration of Gibbs and Martin (1964) and the external constraint theory of Maris (1969).

While the concepts of "anomie," "social isolation," and "normlessness" may be applicable to all blacks who have been uprooted from stable Southern rural to mobile Northern urban or suburban communities, they should predict higher suicide rates for older blacks, for whom the impact of moving to a new environment is arguably even more traumatic than for younger people; yet this is not the case. Furthermore, these sociological theories fail to explain the differential suicide rates of black males and females, who presumably experience similar environmental changes and stressors and yet respond to them very differently.

Second, the psychological perspective can be traced from Freud's psychoanalytic concept that suicide represents anger resulting from the loss of a loved object, turned against the self (Freud, 1917/1925). This concept was further elaborated by Abraham (1927) and others to include suicide as a response to depression, which results from loss of a loved object, loss of self-esteem, or failure to attain desired goals. Contemporary advocates of this viewpoint include Toolan (1975) and Glaser (1978) on youth suicide.

However, as Hendin (1969) points out, the Freudian notion that suicide is a form of inverted homicide due to an "unconscious hostility toward a lost love object" is not supported in clinical treatment of young blacks, who alternately exhibit conscious overt violence and self-destructive behavior as ways of dealing with their underlying feelings of rage and despair. Furthermore, this theory emphasizes the intrapsychic and interpersonal aspects of suicidal behavior at the expense of structural and environmental aspects, which may be even more significant as etiological factors for black youths. For example, Maris (1969) views suicide in black males who have a history of confrontation with authority and/or police records as a response to "retroflexed anger" toward external constraints, rather than a sign of hopelessness or depression.

Third, the ecological perspective, which overlaps the other two perspectives, is advanced by Holinger and Offer (1982), who have used a correlational analysis to show that youth suicide rates increase as the proportion of the 15–24 age group increases in the population. They propose that increased competition for scarcer resources and fewer opportunities results in a cycle of loss of self-esteem, failure, and eventual suicide. The predictive model developed by these researchers appears to be more applicable to white youths than to black youths, suggesting that there are other factors besides population density and competition for limited resources that drive black youths to suicide. On the contrary, the model should be even more powerful for blacks, since even in times of economic prosperity and increased opportunities, black youths still experience high rates of unemployment and other negative social indicators (Gibbs, 1984).

The ecological approach also can be extended to include the theory of urban stress—that is, the notion that black youths are particularly vulnerable to suicide because of high rates of unemployment, dysfunctional families, police brutality, racism, and chaotic environments (Breed, 1970; Bush, 1976; Seiden, 1972). These conditions produce high levels of frustration and hostility, resulting either in suicide or in homicidal behavior through self-destructive risk taking or criminal activities (Grier & Cobbs, 1968).

These ecological factors alone do not seem to account for the suicide rates in black youths. For example, even though the unemployment rate for black youths aged 16–19 quadrupled between 1960 and 1983 (from 12.1% to 48.5%), the suicide rate for females in that age group was nearly the same, and the rate for males only slightly more than doubled in that same time period. However, the peak suicide rates for black youths in the past 25 years have occurred in 1967, 2 years after the passage of major civil rights legislation and urban riots; in 1971–1972, 2 years after the demise of the poverty program and the beginning of the Nixon administration; and in 1976–1977, at the end of the Nixon–Ford era. This suggests the concept of relative deprivation as a moderating factor in black youth suicide; that is, as the gap widens between their rising aspirations and their opportunities to achieve them, they become more angry and frustrated, internalizing their rage and directing it back on themselves.

This brief critique of three conceptual perspectives on black youth suicide suggests the need for a multiple-factor interdisciplinary theory to explain and predict suicidal behavior in black youths. Such a theory should include societal factors (e.g., status integration, norms, etc.), psychological factors (e.g., self-esteem, impulse control, coping mechanisms, etc.), social-psychological factors (e.g., aspirations, risk-taking attitudes, etc.), and ecological factors (e.g., demographic trends, opportunity structures, social supports, etc.). For example, no single-factor theory can explain why suicide rates among black youths are so much lower than among whites; why male rates are so much higher than female rates; or why black suicide decreases with age, while white suicide increases. However, a more complex theory, such as those proposed by Maris (1985) and Bush (1976), would take into account both the factors that foster suicidal behavior (e.g., lack of social integration, unsublimated anger, unfulfilled aspirations, and limited opportunities) as well as those factors that mitigate against it (e.g., extended family networks, strong religious beliefs, alternative value systems, and alternative opportunity structures).

Sociocultural Factors in Differential Suicide Rates

As noted earlier, suicide rates of black youths have traditionally been much lower than those of white youths, in spite of their obvious exposure to greater external stresses of discrimination, poverty, and marginal minority status in American society. However, as the suicide rates of black youths have gradually increased in the past 25 years, it is crucial to identify those sociocultural factors that have contributed to low rates, and, conversely, those that may have fostered increased rates of suicidal behavior in this group.

Those factors that have immunized black youths against suicide can be characterized as "protective factors," in Rutter's (1985) term. Scholars have identified five major institutions that characterized the traditional segregated black community: the strong family; the church; fraternal and social organizations; community schools; and extended kin and social support networks (Allen, 1978; Billingsley, 1968; Martin & Martin, 1978; McAdoo, 1981; Stack, 1974). These institutions promoted a sense of social cohesion, shared values, and mutual support, all of which mitigated against high suicide rates.

Since blacks migrated from the South in the 1930s and 1940s and left those traditional communities, these institutions have been significantly weakened through urbanization, integration, and massive social and economic change. These changes have been accompanied by an increase in the "risk factors" for black youths (and blacks in general) that make them more vulnerable to suicide: (1) the breakdown in family structure, so that 42% of all black families are now female-headed (48% of those households with children under 18 are female-headed); (2) the decreased influence of the church and religious values among urban blacks, especially youths; (3) the declining impact of fraternal and social organizations as middle-class blacks have moved out of the central cities; (4) the deterioration of inner-city schools as they have lost resources, personnel, and middle-class students; and (5) the weakening of social support systems as unemployment and welfare dependency have sapped the dignity, initiative, and aspirations of inner-city residents (Clark, 1965; Glasgow, 1981; Schulz, 1969).

Although these "risk factors" are useful in accounting for suicide among low-income, inner-city youths as in the case of Robert, they are not very applicable to the suicidal behavior of black middle-class youths. As recent newspaper articles and television programs have noted, upwardly mobile black high school students are caught between parental pressures for them to achieve and peer pressures for them to conform to anti-intellectual norms. Black college students in integrated colleges have generally felt relegated to a very marginal role in social and extracurricular activities, but more recently have become targets of overt verbal and physical racial attacks at campuses as diverse as the University of Massachusetts, the University of Michigan, Dartmouth College, and The Citadel. Young professional blacks with impeccable educational credentials have found their careers sidetracked and derailed in major corporations, law firms, and financial institutions. As in the case of Karen, they have internalized the Protestant work ethic and accepted the challenges of integration, only to find that true assimilation into the mainstream is a myth, that they will always be "outsiders"—marginal persons who can play on the field but will never manage the team.

The concept of relative deprivation seems most useful in understanding why more middle-class and upper-middle-class black youths appear to be committing suicide. The civil rights movement of the 1960s and 1970s raised their hopes and aspirations that they would have opportunities limited only by their ability and motivation. When their expectations have failed to materialize, they have become frustrated, angry, and bitter. Some have dropped out of the race, while others have succumbed to depression and despair. In clinical situations, they alternately express their feelings of failure and loss of self-confidence, on the one hand, and their feelings of betrayal and anger at the system, on the other (Gibbs, 1975; Grier & Cobbs, 1968).

Similarly, this set of risk factors does not adequately explain the differential suicide rates of young black males and females. Since both sexes are presumably exposed to the same "protective" and "risk" factors (e.g., family structures, societal forces, and cultural values), what factors and concepts might account for the greater vulnerability of black males to commit suicide? Although this is not a simple question to answer, some clues can be found in an analysis of several social indicators, which suggest that young black males are at significantly higher risk than black females for a number of deviant and self-destructive behaviors. Black males are more likely than black females to be suspended or expelled from school, to be high school dropouts, to be arrested for delinquency or criminal activity, to be substance abusers, to be unemployed, and to be incarcerated (Gibbs, 1984). They are also more likely to die as a result of homicide or accidents. In fact, the two leading causes of death for black males and females aged 15–24 were homicide and motor vehicle accidents, but male rates per 100,000 exceeded female rates in both categories by a ratio of 4:1 (U.S. DHHS, 1986).

A recent study of black male mortality in California from 1978 to 1982 predicted that, if the death rate of this group were to remain unchanged, then 1 in 20 (or 5%) of black males born in California during that period would eventually die from a gun-related fatal injury (U.S. DHHS, 1986). Projections from national homicide statistics for black males confirm this alarming figure. In their study of trends in suicidal methods, McIntosh and Santos (1982) noted that the use of firearms increased for blacks from 50% in the 1920s to 60% in the 1970s, and that it was the method most frequently used by black males throughout this period. In addition, black males are much more likely to be victims of police brutality or killed in confrontations with police than are whites (Pierce, 1986). Finally, young black male drug abusers are in one of the highest risk groups for acquired immune deficiency syndrome (AIDS), accounting for 25% of the new cases between 1983 and 1986 (Morgan & Curran, 1986). While it is estimated that 35.3% of AIDS cases in black males are due to use of unsterile needles for intravenous drug use, the increase of AIDS among black females has occurred primarily as a result of sexual contact with infected heterosexual and bisexual drug abusers. Thus, the fact that black males engage in and are exposed to more self-destructive and violent activities than black females results in a more noxious and dangerous environment for them, placing them at greater risk for negative outcomes physically, psychologically, and socially.

In addition, some literature suggests that black families and other institutions provide differential levels of support and positive reinforcement for black male and female children and adolescents. For example, ethnographic and sociological studies of black families show that boys are disciplined more harshly, trained for independence earlier, and positively reinforced for adolescent aggression and sexuality (Allen, 1978; Schulz, 1969). Black females, on the other hand, receive more nurturance, later independence training, less reinforcement for adolescent aggression, and more reinforcement for academic achievement than males (Bartz & Levine, 1978; Peters, 1981).

These differential child-rearing strategies of black parents toward their male and female children have been linked to different behavioral outcomes in psychological research. If, as Erikson (1950) proposes, the major tasks of adolescence are to develop a sense of personal identity, to establish a clear gender identity, to establish autonomy from parents, and to develop educational or vocational goals, then black females appear to be more successful than black males in negotiating these developmental tasks. Although the results are not totally consistent, the bulk of the psychological research comparing black male and female adolescents on a number of dimensions indicates that black females have higher self-esteem and self-concept (as a measure of positive identity), are less conflicted about their gender identity (black males tend to score high on feminine attributes), have a higher need for independence on psychological scales, and have higher educational and vocational aspirations than black males (Gibbs, 1985; Smith, 1982).

Not only do black males and females receive differential treatment from parents and family members, but schools and other institutions also reinforce this treatment. As noted earlier, black male students have higher suspension, expulsion, and dropout rates than black females. Black males also have more confrontations with the police and are treated more harshly by the juvenile justice system. Young black females can find part-time and full-time employment more easily than black males, perhaps because they are perceived as having more positive attitudes and better work habits. To summarize, black males and females are the objects of differential patterns of socialization from their earliest years in their families; differential reinforcement by teachers in schools; and differential treatment by police, employers, and other gatekeepers of society. This pervasive and persistent differential treatment results in less nurturance, fewer social supports, lower levels of positive reinforcement, more social and economic discrimination, and fewer opportunities for social mobility for black males as compared to black females in our society. Since all of these factors have been theoretically and empirically linked in the literature to youth suicide, it follows that black males are at much higher risk than black females for suicidal behavior (Frederick, 1984).

Implications for Assessment and Early Intervention

What implications for assessment and early intervention can be drawn from the use of a multiple-factor model of suicidal behavior in black youths? In terms of evaluating suicidal risk, clinicians should focus their attention on three aspects of assessment. First, there are sociocultural differences in the expression of depression and/or suicidal intent; that is, black youths are more likely to be verbally abusive, to report somatic symptoms, to express sullen or hostile affect, to fail or act out in school, and to have very conflictual relationships with peers (Grier & Cobbs, 1968; Hendin, 1969; Smith & Carter, 1986). Second, persistent risk taking, involvement in sexual promiscuity, substance abuse, and delinquency in black youths are behaviors that may signal feelings of alienation, hopelessness, and despair, often resulting in self-destructive activities or violent confrontations with the police (Gibbs, 1982). Third, the accumulation of life stress indicators should be noted, including such factors as loss of a parent by death or divorce; poverty; frequent mobility; chronic health problems; child abuse; parental unemployment; and parental history of psychiatric disorder, substance abuse, or criminal behavior. Since the majority of black youths are from lower-income families, they are more likely than white youths to experience a higher number of these life stress indicators, which are also known correlates of suicide in young people (Children's Defense Fund, 1986; Cohen-Sandler, Berman, & King, 1982; Grueling & DeBlassie, 1980; Hendin, 1969; Ladame & Jeanneret, 1982). Fourth, for middle-class black youths, special attention should be paid to dramatic changes in behavior and affect (e.g., moodiness, irritability, crying spells), social relationships (withdrawal, rejection of former friends), and school or job performance (underachievement, absenteeism, lack of motivation). Such changes may be a response to recent social rejection, failed educational aspirations, or blocked career mobility, resulting in a loss of self-esteem, feelings of hopelessness and helplessness, and subsequent suicidal behavior.

Since the presuicidal behaviors of many black youths will be identified initially in school, medical, social welfare, and juvenile justice settings rather than in psychiatric settings, it is imperative for professionals such as doctors, teachers, and social workers (as well as psychiatrists and psychologists) to familiarize themselves with behavioral signs, physical symptoms, and life stress indicators, which are heavily influenced by the social and cultural context of young blacks' lives.

Next, what are the implications for early intervention to prevent depression or self-destructive behaviors from deteriorating into suicidal behavior? Numerous suggestions have been advocated to improve early detection and provide suicide prevention services for youths, but Seiden (1972) and others have proposed several that are particularly relevant to black youths. First, comprehensive clinics should be located in inner-city high schools to provide improved access to health and mental health services for black youths. Second, suicide prevention services should be located in inner-city neighborhoods, and these services should develop aggressive community outreach programs, employ minority-group staff members, and operate 24-hour hotlines (Seiden, 1972). Third, black youths who are identified as at high risk for suicidal behavior should be referred for individual and family counseling and whatever social, educational, economic, or medical services they may require. Fourth, police and community relations should be improved to alleviate the tensions between black youths and the police. This would include hiring more black police officers, setting up police review boards, and providing strong sanctions against police brutality toward inner-city blacks (Seiden, 1972).

Fifth, young black males from fatherless homes need positive male role models to teach them appropriate "masculine" behaviors and values as alternatives to delinquency and violence. Similarly, young black females need positive female role models to show them alternative routes to adulthood other than teenage pregnancy (Gibbs, 1986; Ladner, 1971). Organizations like Big Brothers and Big Sisters should recruit more black adults as volunteers for these programs. Sixth, gun control legislation is badly needed to reduce the availability of lethal weapons in order to prevent suicide as well as homicide among black youths.

Finally, early intervention may increase the probability that some high-risk youths will be prevented from committing suicide, but it is not clear that it prevents the majority of suicide in this age group. More empirical research is needed to test the sometimes conflicting conceptual theories of black youth suicide, in order to develop early intervention programs that are appropriately designed to target this heterogeneous group. These early intervention efforts can only be effective if they are developed within a relevant conceptual framework that addresses the interaction among sociocultural factors, ecological forces, situational events, and individual coping strategies in these black youths. The ultimate solution is primary prevention, and, for black youths this would mean a total restructuring of society to eliminate racism and poverty; a comprehensive family policy to strengthen black families; a federal full-employment and youth employment policy to provide meaningful jobs and adequate incomes to black males; and societal commitment to equality of opportunity and equal administration of justice (Edelman, 1987; Moynihan, 1986).

Without such fundamental changes in American society, the external stresses (poverty, dysfunctional families, discrimination) and the internal stresses (feelings of alienation, frustration, anger, depression) impinging on black youths will produce an intolerable level of stress, with a presumably predictable increase in suicide rates. As long as black youths perceive the wide gap between the American dream of success and the barriers to their achievement of this goal, they will be extremely vulnerable to the twin tragedies of suicide (anger turned inward) and homicide (anger turned outward). In closing, let me quote a brief poem, "Harlem," by the noted black poet, Langston Hughes.[3] It sums up the situation of black youths in contemporary American society poignantly and powerfully:

> What happens to a dream deferred?
>   Does it dry up
>   like a raisin in the sun?
>   Or fester like a sore—
>   And then run?
>   Does it stink like rotten meat?
>   Or crust and sugar over—
>   like a syrupy sweet?
>
>   Maybe it just sags
>   like a heavy load.
>
>   Or does it explode?

---

[3] Copyright 1951 by Langston Hughes. Reprinted from *Selected Poems of Langston Hughes*, by Langston Hughes, by permission of Alfred A. Knopf, Inc.

References

Abraham, K. *Selected papers of Karl Abraham*. New York: Basic Books, 1927.

Allen, W. R. Black family research in the United States: A review, assessment and extension. *Journal of Comparative Family Studies*, 1978, *9*, 168–189.

Aponte, R., Neckerman, R., & Wilson, W. J. *Race, family structure and social policy* (Working Paper 7: Race and Policy). Washington, D.C.: National Council on Social Welfare, 1985.

Bartz, K. W., & Levine, E. S. Childrearing by black parents: A description and comparison to Anglo and Chicano parents. *Journal of Marriage and the Family*, 1978, *40*, 709–719.

Billingsley, A. *Black families in white America*. Englewood Cliffs, NJ: Prentice-Hall, 1968.

Breed, W. The Negro and fatalistic suicide. *Pacific Sociological Review*, 1970, *13*, 156–162.

Bush, J. A. Suicide and blacks: A conceptual framework. *Suicide and Life-Threatening Behavior*, 1976, *6*, 216–222.

Children's Defense Fund. *A children's defense budget*. Washington, D.C.: Author, 1986.

Clark, K. *Dark ghetto*. New York: Harper & Row, 1965.

Cohen-Sandler, R., Berman, A., & King, R. Life stress and symptomatology: Determinants of suicidal behavior in children. *Journal of the American Academy of Child Psychiatry*, 1982, *21*, 178–186.

Durkheim, E. *Suicide*. New York: Free Press, 1962. (Originally published, 1897.)

Edelman, M. W. *Families in peril: An agenda for social change*. Cambridge, MA: Harvard University Press, 1987.

Erikson, E. *Childhood and society*. New York: Norton, 1950.

Frederick, C. J. (1984). Suicide in young minority group persons. In H. Sudak, A. Ford, & N. Rushforth (Eds.), *Suicide in the young*. Boston: John Wright & Sons.

Freud, S. Mourning and melancholia. In *Collected papers of Sigmund Freud* (Vol. 4). London: Hogarth Press, 1925. (Originally published, 1917.)

Gibbs, J. P., & Martin, W. T. *Status integration and suicide*. Eugene: University of Oregon Press, 1964.

Gibbs, J. T. Use of mental health services by black students at a predominantly white university: A three-year study. *American Journal of Orthopsychiatry*, 1975, *45*, 430–445.

Gibbs, J. T. Depression and suicidal behavior among delinquent females: Ethnic and sociocultural variations. *Journal of Clinical Psychology*, 1982, *38*, 159–167.

Gibbs, J. T. Black adolescents and youth: An endangered species. *American Journal of Orthopsychiatry*, 1984, *54*, 6–21.

Gibbs, J. T. City girls: Psychosocial adjustment of urban black adolescent females. *SAGE: A Scholarly Journal on Black Women*, 1985, *2*, 28–36. (a)

Gibbs, J. T. Psychosocial factors associated with depression in urban adolescent females: Implications for assessment. *Journal of Youth and Adolescence*, 1986, *14*, 47–60. (b)

Glaser, K. The treatment of depressed and suicidal adolescents. *American Journal of Psychotherapy*, 1978, *32*, 252–269.

Glasgow, D. *The black underclass*. New York: Vintage Books, 1981.

Grier, W., & Cobbs, P. *Black rage*. New York: Basic Books, 1968.

Grueling, J. W., & DeBlassie, R. R. Adolescent suicide. *Adolescence*, 1980, *59*, 589–601.

Hendin, H. Black suicide. *Archives of General Psychiatry*, 1969, *21*, 407–422.

Holinger, P. C., & Offer, D. Prediction of adolescent suicide: A population model. *American Journal of Psychiatry*, 1982, *139*, 302–307.

Hughes, L. *Selected poems of Langston Hughes*. New York: Knopf, 1981.

Ladame, F., & Jeanneret, O. (1982). Suicide in adolescence: Some comments on epidemiology and prevention. *Journal of Adolescence*, *5*, 355–366.

Ladner, J. (1971). *Tomorrow's tomorrow*. Garden City, N.Y.: Doubleday, 1971.

Maris, R. W. *Social forces in urban suicide.* Homewood, Ill.: Dorsey Press, 1969.
Maris, R. W. The adolescent suicide problem. *Suicide and Life-Threatening Behavior,* 1985, *15*(2), 91–109.
Martin, E., & Martin, J. *The black extended family.* Chicago: University of Chicago Press, 1978.
McAdoo, H. (Ed.). *Black families.* Beverly Hills, CA: Sage, 1981.
McIntosh, J. L., & Santos, J. F. Changing patterns in methods of suicide by race and sex. *Suicide and Life-Threatening Behavior,* 1982, *12,* 221–233.
Morgan, W. M., & Curran, J. W. Acquired immunodeficiency syndrome: Current and future trends. *Public Health Reports,* 1986, *101,* 462–465.
Moynihan, D. P. *Family and nation.* New York: Harcourt Brace Jovanovich, 1986.
National Institute on Drug Abuse (NIDA) (1985). *Drug abuse among minorities.* Rockville, MD: Alcohol, Drug Abuse and Mental Health Administration.
Ozawa, M. N. Nonwhites and the demographic imperative in social wlfare spending. *Social Work,* 1986, *31,* 440–447.
Peters, M. F. Parenting in black families with young children: A historical perspective. In H. McAdoo (Ed.), *Black families.* Beverly Hills, CA: Sage, 1981.
Pierce, H. P. Blacks and law enforcement: Toward police brutality reduction. *The Black Scholar,* 1986, *17,* 49–54.
Rutter, M. Resilience in the face of adversity. *British Journal of Psychiatry,* 1985, *147,* 598–611.
Schulz, D. A. *Coming up black: Patterns of ghetto socialization.* Englewood Cliffs, NJ: Prentice-Hall, 1969.
Seiden, R. H. Why are suicides of young blacks increasing? *H.S.M.H.S. Health Reports,* 1972, *87,* 3–8.
Shaffer, D., & Fisher, P. The epidemiology of suicide in children and young adolescents. *Journal of the American Academy of Child Psychiatry,* 1981, *20,* 545–565.
Smart, R. G. Drug abuse among adolescents and self-destructive behavior. In N. L. Farberow (Ed.), *The many faces of suicide.* New York: McGraw-Hill, 1980.
Smith, E. The black female adolescent: A review of the educational, career and psychological literature. *Psychology of Women Quarterly,* 1982, *6,* 261–288.
Smith, J. A., & Carter, J. H. Suicide and black adolescents: A medical dilemma. *Journal of the National Medical Association,* 1986, *78,* 1061–1064.
Stack, C. *All our kin.* New York: Harper & Row, 1974.
Taube, C. A., & Barrett, S. A. (Eds.). *Mental health, United States, 1985* (DHHS Publication No. NIMH 85-1378). Washington, D.C.: U.S. Government Printing Office, 1985.
Toolan, J. M. Suicide in children and adolescents. *American Journal of Psychotherapy,* 1975, *29,* 339–344.
U.S. Bureau of the Census. *Statistical abstract of the United States* (106th ed.). Washington, D.C.: U.S. Government Printing Office, 1986.
U.S. Department of Health and Human Services (DHHS). *Health, United States, 1985* (DHHS Publication No. PHS 86-1232). Washington, D.C.: U.S. Government Printing Office, 1985.
U.S. Department of Health and Human Services (DHHS). *Report of the secretary's task force on black and minority health, Vol. 5.* Washington, D.C.: U.S. Government Printing Office, 1986.
Warshauer, M., & Monk, M. Problems in suicide statistics for whites and blacks. *American Journal of Public Health,* 1978, *68,* 383–388.

CHAPTER 9

The Impact of Suicide in Television Movies: Replication and Commentary

Madelyn S. Gould, PhD, MPH, David Shaffer, MD, and Marjorie Kleinman, MA

Columbia University College of Physicians and Surgeons
New York State Psychiatric Institute

Most of the research on imitative suicide has focused on the reporting of nonfictional suicides in the mass media (Baron & Reiss, 1985; Barraclough, Shepherd, & Jennings, 1977; Blumenthal & Bergner, 1973; Bollen & Phillips, 1981, 1982; Littmann, 1985; Motto, 1967, 1970; Phillips, 1974, 1979, 1980; Phillips & Carstensen, 1986; Stack, 1984; Wasserman, 1984) Little research has been carried out on the impact of fictional stories, and the few recent studies have proven controversial, with findings of significant imitative effects (Holding, 1974, 1975; Schmidtke & Hafner, 1986), no imitative effects (Berman, 1986, 1987; Phillips & Paight, 1987), and sex- and age-specific imitative effects (Platt, 1987).

Last year, we (Gould & Shaffer, 1986) published a paper on the impact of television broadcasts of fictional stories featuring suicidal behavior that suggested that an increase in teenage suicides followed the broadcasts. The variation in youth suicide and attempted suicide was examined in the greater New York metropolitan area before and after four fictional television films broadcast in the fall and winter of 1984–1985. The study examined a consecutive series of 31 completed suicides of youths aged 19 and under, which had occurred during the period from September 15, 1984, through March 9, 1985, in New York

Requests for reprints should be sent to Dr. Madelyn S. Gould, Division of Child Psychiatry, Columbia University College of Physicians and Surgeons, 722 West 168th Street, New York, NY 10032. This work was supported in part by a Faculty Scholar's Award from the William T. Grant Foundation and a research grant (No. MH38198) from the National Institute of Mental Health. This chapter is based in part on an address given at the joint meeting of the American Association of Suicidology and the International Association for Suicide Prevention, San Francisco, May 1987.

City and 28 surrounding counties in New York State, New Jersey, and Connecticut. The study area represented 3 million youths aged 10–19, or approximately 7.5% of the U.S. population in this age range. A sample of 220 young people who had attempted suicide and were seen at six New York area hospitals during this time period was also examined. The 25-week period of time extended from 1 month before the first television broadcast to 1 month after the fourth television broadcast.

Given the limited sample, we recognized that further study was needed in extending the examination to other geographic areas. This chapter presents current efforts to replicate and expand the original study.

Method

Sample

The criteria for the selection of additional metropolitan areas to be examined were as follows: (1) The cities represented each of the three geographic regions (other than Northeast) specified in the U.S. Census: Midwest (North Central), South, and West; (2) the cities were within the top 25 metropolitan areas (consolidated metropolitan statistical areas, or CMSAs) in the United States (U.S. Bureau of the Census, 1984), so that a large sample of completed suicides could be identified; (3) the broadcast dates of the movies within each city were the same as in the original study. This allowed for at least a 2-week interval between each of the movies. The broadcast dates of one of the movies (an after-school special) varied across the country, with a considerable number of communities not airing the movie.[1]

Three CMSAs met the criteria: Cleveland–Akron–Lorain, Ohio (Midwest), Dallas–Fort Worth, Texas (South), and Los Angeles–Anaheim–Riverside, California (West).

For each metropolitan area, only counties within the CMSA that were also within the designated market area (DMA) for that region were included in the current examination. This yielded seven counties in the Cleveland area (Cuyahoga, Geauga, Lake, Lorain, Medina, Portage, and Summit); five counties in the Los Angeles area (Los Angeles, Orange, Riverside, San Bernadino, and Ventura); and nine counties in the Dallas area (Collin, Dallas, Denton, Ellis, Johnson, Kaufman, Parker,

---

[1] The broadcast dates of this after-school special were provided by Phillip Harding, Office of Social and Policy Research, CBS.

Rockwall, and Tarrant). A DMA, established by the Nielsen station index, is a geographic area that consists of all the counties in which the home market television stations receive a preponderance of viewing (A. C. Nielsen Company, 1986). The counties within the DMA can be linked to specific TV stations. In this way, it can be determined whether there is an ABC, CBS, or NBC affiliate within the area, and thus whether a particular television movie was available to that area. Inclusion in the DMA also established that acceptable broadcast reception was available for the areas examined.

Source of Data

The state vital statistics offices of Ohio, Texas, and California provided the mortality data for the three additional CMSAs.[2] A comprehensive register of persons who attempted suicide was not established in the three additional geographic areas, as it had been for the original report (Gould & Shaffer, 1986). Therefore, the data are limited to completed suicides by persons 19 years of age or younger.

Results

The number of completed suicides in the 2-week period before and after each of the television movies was broadcast for each of the metropolitan areas is presented in Table 9-1. Consistent with the original report, one suicide story (Broadcast 2) was excluded in the analysis of completed suicides.

The entire set of data was analyzed employing a randomized block factorial analysis of variance (Kirk, 1968). This repeated-measures analytic design utilized the three movies as the blocking factor, with locale and time (i.e., before or after the movies) as the two treatment factors. The results, given in Table 9-2, indicate a significant interaction between geographic area and time. In other words, the impact of the movies was not uniform across all of the cities. Consequently, tests of main effects are of little interest, and attention is directed to tests of the effects of the movies within each city.

---

[2] Data from the National Center for Health Statistics for 1985 were not available in May 1987, when these results were originally presented, nor at the time of the preparation of the present chapter.

TABLE 9-1.   Number of Completed Suicides by Adolescents in New York, Cleveland,
Dallas, and Los Angeles CMSAs

| | Broadcast 1 | | Broadcast 2[a] | | Broadcast 3 | | Broadcast 4 | |
CMSA	Before	After	Before	After	Before	After	Before	After
New York[b]	2	5	—	0	0	4	1	4
Cleveland	1	3	—	1	0	1	2	4
Dallas	1	0	—	0	1	2	2	0
Los Angeles	5	4	—	2	4	1	1	4

[a] Data are provided for Broadcast 2 but were not included in the analyses.
[b] Data from Gould & Shaffer (1986).

Within-City Analysis

For each city, the mean difference in the number of completed suicides
before and after the three television movies was compared employing
a paired t-test analysis. Greater statistical power is derived from the
paired t test because it accounts for the correlation between the premovie
and postmovie number of suicides. As expected from the original report,
there was a significant excess in the number of completed suicides in
the New York region following the movies, t (2) = 9.99, $p < .01$, two-
tailed. There was no significant difference between the mean number
of completed suicides before or after the three television broadcasts in
the Dallas and Los Angeles regions. In the Cleveland area, the number
of completed suicides after the three broadcasts ($M = 2.67, SD = 1.53$)
was significantly greater than the mean number before the broadcasts
($M = 1, SD = 1$), t (2) = 5.0, $p = .038$, two-tailed. If a Bonferroni t

TABLE 9-2.   Results of the Analysis of Variance for Completed
Suicides by Adolescents in New York, Cleveland, Dallas,
and Los Angeles CMSAs

Source	df	F	p
Blocks (movies)	2	1.23	
Treatments			
Time (pre–post)	1	3.61	.078
City	3	3.28	.052
City × time	3	3.15	.059[a]
Residual	14	—	—

[a] A level of .059 was considered significant, because the test employing a
fixed-effects model was negatively biased (Kirk, 1968) and the power to detect
a signficant effect was quite small, given the current design (Cohen, 1977).

procedure is applied, then the difference is significant between the .05 and .10 levels. Because each control period preceded the experimental period, the possibility existed that the significant increase in suicides after the broadcasts merely reflected a tendency for suicides to increase over time. Therefore, a second analysis was performed that used a 2-year period (1984 and 1985, n = 59 suicides) to derive an expected number of suicides during the period following the broadcasts. The observed number of suicides that occurred during the three 2-week periods following the movies (8, or 13.6% of the total number of suicides), was significantly greater than expected (3.4, or 5.8%; p = .01, based on the binomial distribution).

Further analyses were conducted for the Cleveland area to rule out alternative explanations for the excess of completed suicides after the broadcasts.

Weekly Trends

A possibility existed that the analysis may have reflected an increase that was inherent to the experimental periods, quite independent from an effect of the movies. In this case, a significant increase in suicides would be expected in comparable "experimental" weeks in years in which the broadcasts were not aired. For the Cleveland area, the 6-year period prior to the movie year was examined (see Table 9-3). There was no significant difference in the number of suicides in the "experimental" periods (M = 1.1, SD = .42) and "control" periods (M = 1.3, SD = .15) for the pooled years or for any single year.[3] The excess in completed suicides occurred only in the year in which the movies were broadcast.

Acceleration

The increase following the broadcasts in Cleveland may have reflected an acceleration of cases that would have occurred soon anyway. If this were so, then the number of suicides in a longer follow-up period should be less than expected. The longer-term drop in suicides would reflect

---

[3] A comparable examination in the New York area will have to await adequate data for New York City. The data for the 6-year period prior to the movie year were available only from state vital statistics or the National Center for Health Statistics. These data sources were inadequate in New York City because, as discussed later in the text, they tend to underreport statistics obtained from the medical examiner's office, as indicated in a review of 1985 and 1986 data.

TABLE 9-3. Number of Completed Suicides by Adolescents in the Cleveland CMSA
for the Comparison Weeks in the 6 Years Prior to the Movies

	Period 1		Period 2[a]		Period 3		Period 4	
	Before	After	Before	After	Before	After	Before	After
1978–1979	3	1	—	2	4	2	3	1
1979–1980	0	0	—	0	1	2	1	0
1980–1981	2	1	—	2	0	0	1	1
1981–1982	2	1	—	1	0	1	1	2
1982–1983	1	0	—	1	2	2	1	1
1983–1984	1	1	—	0	0	0	1	4

[a] Data are provided but were not included in the analyses.

the cases that had "moved up" to the experimental periods, shortly
after the movies. The total movie or experimental period was defined
as October 16 (the date of the first broadcast) through February 23 (2
weeks following the last broadcast). The follow-up period was defined
as February 24 through October 15. The 6-year period prior to the
movies was employed to derive the expected number of suicides in the
movie period and follow-up period. The observed number of suicides
during the movie period (17) was larger than expected (10), whereas
the observed number of suicides in the follow-up period (16) was not
significantly different than expected (17.2). The pattern of results was
not consistent with an acceleration hypothesis. Rather, it suggested
that following the broadcasts there were suicides that would not have
otherwise occurred.

Discussion

The impact of the television broadcasts of fictional stories featuring
suicidal behavior appears less widespread than we had originally proposed. The present results indicated a significant interaction by location,
with a significant excess of suicides following the broadcasts in the
New York and Cleveland regions, but not in the Dallas or Los Angeles
areas.

Recently, Phillips and Paight (1987) published results indicating
that there was no significant effect of the same movies in the states of
California and Pennsylvania. These results are not inconsistent with
the present findings, in that both sets of results might be explained by
an interaction between the locations where the films were shown and
the effect of the films. This is not an unreasonable supposition, because

the way in which the broadcasts were presented varied according to location. The affiliates were encouraged to develop local education programs to go along with the film, and these varied in intensity. Phillips and Paight (1987) have hypothesized that there is a dose–response effect between suicide and the media: More exposure produces more effect. If this is true, it might explain regional variation. However, the extent of affiliate coverage in the areas studied has not been documented. Clearly, the sets of local circumstances have to be examined in detail in future studies to explain the variable impact of the movies.

There are a number of factors that limit the ability of investigations to detect a significant effect of the media or are sources of variability between studies. These include low statistical power, different sources of data, variability in broadcast reception, and differing control periods. Given the small number of completed suicides and a small number of stimuli (i.e., broadcasts), the statistical power to detect a significant effect even when it exists is low. For example, the power to detect a significant effect on completed suicides in our original report (Gould & Shaffer, 1986) was less than .15, assuming a medium effect of the media (Cohen, 1977). One of the advantages of our original study was that the number of examined cases was increased by extending the study to suicide attempts. The fact that identical trends were found in both completions and attempts, and that the effect was repeated after three out of four broadcasts offer suggestive internal replication as well as increasing the power of the analysis. Another means of increasing the number of examined cases might be to include some motor vehicle "accidents" in future examinations. In the likelihood that single-car, single-occupant motor vehicle mortalities are "disguised suicides" (Phillips, 1979), it might be useful to examine the variability of these types of deaths as a function of media events. The inclusion of these deaths should yield increased power to detect a significant effect that might otherwise be missed.

Variability in the completeness of case identification among different sources of data could have an impact on the likelihood of finding a significant effect. For example, an examination of data from the national and state vital statistics and local medical examiner's office in the New York area highlighted a discrepancy, in that cases identified in the local data did not appear in the state or national data. It appears that pending cases may receive verdicts after the deadline for submitting data to the state vital statistics, and that these cases may never be submitted for entry into the national mortality tapes. Because the incidence of suicide is low, the deletion of even a few cases could preclude the detection of a significant effect. The extent to which this inconsistency in data exists in other geographic areas has implications for the adequacy of the data sources and needs to be further examined.

The major limitation of the studies examining the impact of media coverage of suicides is that all have employed aggregate data. In light of the constraints of such a design, the investigations are obligated at the very least to insure that the movies are broadcast in the geographic regions under study. The use of DMAs, as used in the present study, can address this issue. There can be a problem in examining statewide data (e.g., Phillips & Paight, 1987). Because television coverage for the major networks varies in different nonurban locations, whereas it is quite uniform in urban areas, use of statewide data can introduce "noise" and diminish the ability of the study to adequately examine the impact of the media.

The estimation of a stable expectation or baseline number of suicides is necessary for comparison to the experimental period(s). It is not sufficient to limit the examination to weeks before and after the broadcast. As previously noted, because each control period precedes the experimental period, the possibility exists that a significant increase (or decrease) in suicides after the broadcasts may merely reflect a tendency for suicides to increase (or decrease) over time. The examination of one alternative year as the comparison period may also be misleading, because circumstances unknown to the investigator may have yielded a high (or low) incident comparison year. The employment of several comparison years is preferable in establishing a stable estimate of the expected number of suicides.

No one study or few studies will be able to provide conclusive evidence on the impact of the media on suicide. The present results provide another bit of evidence, but should still be considered tentative until the national data are examined. In a future examination of the national data, the impact of the location where the movies were shown should not be overlooked, particularly because large regions without an effect could overshadow small areas with the effect. The evidence from continuing research efforts will have to evaluated. In this light, it is useful to present criteria that assist judgments about the causal significance of associations (Susser, 1973): (1) time sequence of variables (in other words, there is evidence that the increase in mortality occurred only after the media events); (2) consistency of association on replication; (3) strength of association (the stronger the association, the more likely it is to be causal); and (4) coherent explanation (in other words, the association supports pre-existing knowledge and is coherent with other known facts about the outcome and the causal factor). Applying these criteria, Gould and Davidson (1988) have concluded that evidence forcefully supports the existence of imitative suicides following media coverage of nonfictional suicides. Although there is evidence that fictional suicide stories can have a negative impact (Gould & Shaffer, 1986; Holding, 1974, 1975; Schmidtke & Hafner, 1986), there is clearly a need to engage in further careful research in this area to resolve the issue.

References

Baron, J. N., & Reiss, P. C. Reply to Phillips and Bollen. *American Sociological Review*, 1985, *50*, 372–376.

Barraclough, B., Shepherd, D., & Jennings, C. Do newspaper reports of coroners' inquests incite people to commit suicide? *British Journal of Psychiatry*, 1977, *131*, 259–532.

Berman, A. L. *Mass media and youth suicide prevention*. Paper presented at the National Conference on Prevention and Interventions in Youth Suicide, Department of Health and Human Services Task Force on Youth Suicide, Oakland, Calif., 1986.

Berman, A. L. *Fictional suicide and imitation effects*. Paper presented at the meeting of the American Association of Suicidology, San Francisco, May 1987.

Blumenthal, S., & Bergner, L. Suicide and newspaper: A replicated study. *American Journal of Psychiatry*, 1973, *130*, 468–471.

Bollen, K. A., & Phillips, D. P. Suicidal motor vehicle fatalities in Detroit: A replication. *American Journal of Sociology*, 1981, *87*, 404–412.

Bollen, K. A., & Phillips, D. P. Imitative suicides: A national study of the effects of television news stories. *American Sociological Review*, 1982, *47*, 802–809.

Cohen, J. *Statistical power analysis for the behavioral sciences*. New York: Academic Press, 1977.

Gould, M. S., & Davidson, L. Suicide contagion among adolescents. In A. R. Stiffman & R. A. Feldman (Eds.), *Advances in adolescent mental health: Vol. 3. Depression and suicide*. Greenwich, CT: JAI Press, 1988.

Gould, M. S., & Shaffer, D. The impact of suicide in television movies: Evidence of imitation. *New England Journal of Medicine*, 1986, *315*, 690–694.

Holding, T. A. The B.B.C. "Befrienders" series and its effects. *British Journal of Psychiatry*, 1974, *124*, 470–472.

Holding, T. A. Suicide and "The Befrienders." *British Medical Journal*, 1975, *3*, 751–753.

Kirk, R. E. *Experimental design: Procedures for the behavioral sciences*. Belmont, CA: Brooks/Cole, 1968.

Littmann, S. K. Suicide epidemics and newspaper reporting. *Suicide and Life-Threatening Behavior*, 1985, *15*, 43–50.

Motto, J. A. Suicide and suggestibility—the role of the press. *American Journal of Psychiatry*, 1967, *124*, 252–256.

Motto, J. A. Newspaper influence on suicide. *Archives of General Psychiatry*, 1970, *23*, 143–148.

A. C. Nielsen Company. *DMA Test Market Profiles: Media/Marketing Information by Designated Market Areas (DMA)*. New York: Author, 1986.

Phillips, D. P. The influence of suggestion on suicide: Substantive and theoretical implications of the Werther effect. *American Sociological Review*, 1974, *39*, 340–354.

Phillips, D. P. Suicide, motor vehicle fatalities, and the mass media: Evidence toward a theory of suggestion. *American Journal of Sociology*, 1979, *84*, 1150–1174.

Phillips, D. P. Airplane accidents, murder, and the mass media: Towards a theory of imitation and suggestion. *Social Forces*, 1980, *58*, 1001–1004.

Phillips, D. P., & Carstensen, L. L. Clustering of teenage suicides after television news stories about suicide. *New England Journal of Medicine*, 1986, *315*, 685–689.

Phillips, D. P. & Paight, D. J. (1987). The impact of televised movies about suicide: A replicative study. *New England Journal of Medicine, 317*, 809–811.
Platt, S. The aftermath of Angie's overdose: Is soap (opera) damaging to your health? *British Medical Journal*, 1987, *294*, 954–957.
Schmidtke, A., & Hafner, H. Die vermittlung von selbstmordmotivation und selbstmordhandlung durch fiktive modelle. *Nervenarzt*, 1986, *57*, 502–510.
Stack, S. *The effect of suggestion on suicide: A reassessment.* Paper presented at the annual meeting of the American Sociological Association, San Antonio, Texas, 1984.
Susser, M. *Causal thinking in the health sciences: Concepts and strategies in epidemiology.* New York: Oxford University Press, 1973.
U.S. Bureau of the Census. *Statistical abstract of the United States, 1985* (105th ed). Washington, D.C.: U.S. Government Printing Office, 1984.
Wasserman, I. M. Imitation and suicide: A reexamination of the Werther effect. *American* *Sociological Review*, 1984, *49*, 427–436.

CHAPTER 10

The Effect of Suicide Stories on Various Demographic Groups, 1968–1985

David P. Phillips, PhD, and Lundie L. Carstensen, MS
University of California at San Diego

In 1774, Johann Wolfgang von Goethe published a romantic novel, *The Sorrows of Young Werther*, in which the hero committed suicide. The book was widely read throughout Europe, and its hero's behavior was apparently imitated. Some people committed suicide while dressed as Werther was; others killed themselves in the same manner as Werther, with a copy of the novel opened to the page describing his suicide. Goethe (who had written the book in part to purge himself of his own suicidal feelings) was taken aback by the effect of his novel. "My friends ... thought that they must transform poetry into reality, imitate a novel like this in real life and, in any case, shoot themselves; and what occurred at first among a few took place later among the general public" (Goethe, quoted in Rose, 1929, p. 24). Alarmed by the apparent effect of the book, authorities banned the novel in parts of Italy, Denmark, and Germany (Gray, 1967; Rose, 1929). Seventy years later, William Farr, the British Registrar General of Births, Deaths, and Marriages, noted, "No fact is better established in science than that suicide (and murder may perhaps be added) is often committed from imitation" (cited by Phelps, 1911; Pell & Watters, 1982).

In 1897, Durkheim acknowledged that imitation may affect suicide, but only in the sense that it precipitates a few suicides that would have occurred very soon anyway, even in the absence of imitation (Durkheim, 1897/1962). He also maintained that, while suicide may precipitate a few deaths, it cannot do so in sufficient numbers to affect

This research was supported in part by a Biomedical Research Support Grant (RR07011-16) from the U.S. Department of Health and Human Services, and by a grant (RL97-G) from the Regents of the University of California.

the social suicide rate. For three-quarters of a century, Durkheim exerted a nearly papal authority in the sociological study of suicide, and his views on imitation displaced earlier concerns about the possibly harmful effects of suicide stories.

For 75 years after Durkheim's influential book, there was no large-scale study of imitative suicide. The few, small-scale studies that were undertaken were inconclusive (Motto, 1967), contradictory (Crawford & Willis, 1966; Seiden, 1968), or susceptible to various explanations other than imitation (Kreitman, Smith, & Tan, 1969; Weiss, 1958).

It was not until 1974 that the first large-scale study of imitative suicide appeared (Phillips, 1974). Phillips examined the fluctuation of U.S. monthly suicides before and after the appearance of heavily publicized suicide stories. Correcting for the effects of seasons and secular trends, he found that U.S. suicides had a statistically significant tendency to increase after suicide stories, by about 58 suicides per story. The more publicity given to the story, the greater the increase in suicides thereafter. The increase in suicides occurred mainly in the geographic areas where the suicide story was publicized. In honor of Goethe's hero, Phillips named the poststory increase in suicides the "Werther effect."

Suicide stories do not appear merely to precipitate suicides that would   λ have occurred anyway. If the "precipitation explanation" were correct, the poststory rise in suicides should be followed by an equally large drop in suicides below the normal level, caused by people "moving up" their death dates. No such drop has been found, and this suggests that Durkheim was incorrect: Suicide stories seem to trigger some deaths that would not have occurred otherwise. Phillips assessed four additional, alternative explanations for his findings, including the possibility that they were due to misclassification or to prior events that triggered both the publicized suicide and the rise in suicides thereafter. He concluded that the best available explanation for his findings was that suicide stories elicit some imitative behavior; the precise nature of these imitative processes was not then (and is not now) understood.

Not all suicides are recorded as such; some may be disguised as automobile accidents, particularly as single-car crashes. If this is so, then automobile accident fatalities should also increase just after publicized suicide stories. Phillips (1977, 1979) found evidence for such increases in a study of daily California motor vehicle fatalities (MVFs) from 1966 to 1973. After correcting for the influence of day of the week, months, holidays, and secular trends, he discovered the following:

1. MVFs increased significantly by 9.12% in the week after a suicide story, with most of this increase being concentrated on the third day, when a 31% rise in MVFs was evident. (A subsequent, replicative

study by Bollen & Phillips, 1981, found a 35% increase in Detroit
MVFs on the third day after suicide stories.)

2. The more publicity the suicide story received, the more MVFs increased just afterwards.

3. The increase was greatest in the areas where the suicide story was
most heavily publicized.

4. The increase was much larger for single-vehicle than for multiple-
vehicle accidents.

5. The drivers in these single-vehicle crashes were unusually similar
to the person described in the suicide story.

6. There was no such similarity between the publicized suicide and
(a) passengers who died just after the story, or (b) drivers who died
in multiple-vehicle crashes just after the story.

It is difficult to generate alternative explanations for these findings;
Phillips concluded that the best available explanation was that suicide
stories trigger some additional suicides, some of which are recorded as
motor vehicle accidents.

   In a study of U.S. monthly suicides, Wasserman (1984) concluded
that suicide stories trigger imitation only if the story concerns a celebrity
suicide. However, Stack (1984) noted that Wasserman had inadvertently
omitted some publicized stories from his analysis; when these stories
were included, Stack found no significant difference between the effect
of celebrity and noncelebrity suicide stories (after correction for the
amount of publicity devoted to each story). We (Phillips, Paight, &
Carstensen, in press) uncovered similar findings with a different data
set. (For a detailed study on the impact of celebrity suicide stories, see
Stack, 1987.)

   The studies reviewed above were typically concerned with the impact
of *newspaper* stories on *monthly* suicides. We (Phillips & Carstensen,
1986) also examined the impact of television network news suicide
stories on daily U.S. suicides from 1973 to 1979. Examination of daily
figures yielded a more detailed picture of the timing and duration of
the suicide peak just after suicide stories. The Werther effect seemed
to persist for 0–7 days after the television story. The peak in suicides
remained statistically significant after corrections for day of the week,
seasons, trends, and holidays.

   In the present study, we sought to broaden the work on television
news stories (Phillips & Carstensen, 1986) in two ways. First, we nearly
tripled the time period under analysis (from 1973–1979 to 1968–1985).
Second, and more important, we analyzed the differential effect of
suicide stories on a wide variety of demographic groups. It is important
to determine whether the effect of suicide stories pervades all segments

Point of research ✓

of society or is concentrated in a few groups. Information of this sort can deepen our understanding of imitative processes and enhance our ability to reduce their harmful consequences; knowing which groups are most affected by suicide stories can help us to target efforts to help them.[1]

Sources and Characteristics of Data under Analysis

The current investigation examined the impact of suicide stories that appeared on network television news programs from 1968 to 1985. The study period began with 1968, because this was the first year covered by the Vanderbilt Television News Index; 1985 was the last year under examination, because computerized California mortality data were not yet available for later years. California mortality tapes were used (in preference to U.S. computerized data) for two reasons. First, information on day of death is available for California for a wider range of years (1960–1985) than it is for the United States as a whole (1973–1984). Second, the California computerized death certificate provides information on the injury date (i.e., the date when the suicidal act began), as well as information on the death date. In contrast, U.S. computerized data record only the death date. Phillips and Sanzone (in press) have found that the relationship between suicide story and a subsequent peak in suicides is slightly weakened when one classifies suicides by date of death rather than by date of injury. This is because there is occasionally a long (and variable) lag between the beginning and end of the suicidal act. Consequently, some persons dying just after the suicide story may have actually begun the suicidal act just before the story appeared. In addition, some persons beginning the suicidal act just after the story may die outside of the period under observation (0–7 days after the story). The effect of these processes is to blur the relationship between a story and the peak thereafter, when the death date (rather than the injury date) is used. For this reason, the current study analyzed mortality by injury date.

Our earlier findings (Phillips & Carstensen, 1986, Table 1) indicated that suicides increased only after suicide stories that were carried on several television programs: After multiprogram suicide stories, teen suicides increased by an average of 5.29 per story ($t = 4.32$, $p = .0003$,

---

[1] This review has been restricted to the impact of nonfictional suicide stories; this has been the primary focus of the literature on imitative suicide. Very recently, researchers have begun to examine the impact of fictional stories as well (see Gould & Shaffer, 1986; Phillips & Paight, 1987; Platt, 1987; Schmidtke & Hafner, 1986).

one-sample two-tailed test, $n = 22$). In strong contrast, teen suicides fell by -0.36 after the average *single*-program story ($t = -0.32$, $p = .75$, one-sample two-tailed test, $n = 16$). The difference between the effect of single-program and multiprogram stories was statistically significant($t = 3.42$, $p = .0015$, two-sample test with approximately 35.8 degrees of freedom). Because of this evidence, the present study examined the impact of multiprogram suicide stories.

These stories were chosen in the following fashion: Multiprogram stories for 1973–1979 were precisely those used earlier (Phillips & Carstensen, 1986). Stories for the remaining years under study (1968–1972, 1980–1985) were chosen from the same television news indexes (CBS News Index, Vanderbilt TV News Index) and according to the same selection criteria used earlier (Phillips & Carstensen, 1986). In addition, we added stories about the "right to die," because stories on this topic have begun to appear under the index heading of suicide in recent years (1980–1985). Stories of this type are likely to become increasingly frequent, and we felt it would be important not to exclude them from this and from future analyses.[2]

Computerized information on California mortality, 1968–1985, was provided by the California Department of Health Services.

Method of Analysis

We used the same time-series regression model employed in earlier work (e.g., Bollen & Phillips, 1982; Phillips & Carstensen, 1986). As in our 1986 study, we sought the effect of a suicide story in the period 0–7 days after its appearance by creating a dummy variable that took the value "1" in this period and "0" elsewhere. In order to correct for the effects of day of the week, month, and year, we created dummy variables for Monday through Saturday, January through November, and 1968 through 1984. In addition, a dummy variable was constructed for each holiday and for each of the days immediately surrounding that holiday. Thus, for instance, we created nine dummy variables for Memorial Day—MEM (-4), MEM (-3), MEM (-2), MEM (-1), MEM (0), MEM (1), MEM (2), MEM (3), MEM (4); another nine dummy variables for July 4th—JUL4 (-4), JUL4 (-3), JUL4 (-2), JUL4 (-1), JUL4 (0), JUL4 (1), JUL4 (2), JUL4 (3), JUL4 (4); and so on, for each of the public holidays. This procedure helped to correct for the impact of

---

[2] Unfortunately, there were only two "right to die" stories listed under the index heading "suicide," so that it is not meaningful to provide a separate analysis of their effects.

holidays on suicide. In addition, we made doubly sure that holiday effects and story effects were not confounded, by omitting a suicide story if the observation period following that story (i.e., 0–7 days after the story) overlapped with a holiday period.

Results

Table 10-1 presents the estimated effect of suicide stories, day of the week, month, year, and holidays on the fluctuation of male and female suicides. We note first that both male and female suicides increased significantly 0–7 days after a publicized suicide story. The coefficient 0.381 indicates that male suicides increased by 0.381 per day in this 8-day observation period, for a total increase of 3.048 male suicides (8 × 0.381) per story. Similarly, female suicides increased by a total of 1.592 (8 × 0.199) per story. Thus, for both sexes combined, California suicides increased by 4.64 (3.048 + 1.592) for each multiprogram suicide story broadcast on network television news programs.[3] Since a total of 43 television news stories were examined, this implies a total increase of 199.52 California suicides after suicide stories. California accounts for about 10% of the U.S. population; if its imitative processes are representative of the United States as a whole, then U.S. suicides increased by a little less than 2,000 after the suicide stories under discussion.

Perhaps the most important finding in Table 10-1 is that the effect of suicide stories was relatively stable over time: The Werther effect remained statistically significant when our original study period (1973–1979) was nearly tripled in size (to 1968–1985).

The remainder of the table reveals patterns similar to those noted elsewhere in the literature. For example, both males and females displayed a significant peak in suicides on Monday. Neither sex showed a very strong seasonal pattern in suicide, but there was some tendency for the level of suicides to be a little higher in spring and early summer. For both sexes, there was a tendency for suicide levels to decline on and immediately before most holidays. There was also a tendency for suicide levels to increase after some holidays, most notably New Year's Day and Labor Day. (For a more detailed analysis of holiday effects, see Phillips & Wills, 1987.) Finally, male and female suicides seemed to be exhibiting different secular trends in California. Male suicides were uniformly lower in the years 1968–1984 than they were in the

---

[3] The appendix to this chapter indicates that these results were not artifacts of autocorrelation or heteroscedasticity.

TABLE 10-1. Fluctuation of California Suicides by Day of Week, Month, and Year, around Holidays, and after Suicide Stories, 1968–1985

Predictor variables	Males Coefficient	t	Females Coefficient	t
Constant	6.726	31.00*	1.921	13.63*
Lag of suicide	0.003	0.25	0.002	0.18
Suicide stories	0.381	2.66*	0.199	2.02*
Monday	0.663	5.46*	0.223	2.67*
Tuesday	0.126	1.03	−0.104	−1.26
Wednesday	0.029	0.24	−0.181	−2.18*
Thursday	0.094	0.77	−0.184	−2.19*
Friday	−0.176	−1.44	−0.036	−0.43
Saturday	−0.430	−3.56*	−0.202	−2.44*
January	0.085	0.48	−0.011	−0.09
February	0.182	1.05	0.117	0.97
March	0.142	0.83	0.223	1.89
April	0.082	0.47	0.219	1.85
May	0.230	1.27	0.385	3.10*
June	0.332	1.90	0.130	1.08
July	0.024	0.13	0.148	1.18
August	−0.056	−0.32	0.208	1.76
September	−0.122	−0.67	0.126	1.01
October	−0.160	−0.93	0.155	1.32
November	−0.066	−0.37	0.125	1.00
New Year's −3 days	0.179	0.29	−0.327	−0.78
New Year's −2 days	−0.636	−1.04	−0.331	−0.79
New Year's −1 day	−0.787	−1.29	−0.996	−2.37*
New Year's Day	0.693	1.11	0.411	0.96
New Year's +1 day	0.216	0.36	−0.641	−1.54
New Year's +2 days	0.752	1.24	0.251	0.60
New Year's +3 days	0.935	1.54	0.915	2.19*
New Year's +4 days	−0.957	−1.58	0.017	0.04
July 4th −4 days	−0.821	−1.35	−0.345	−0.83
July 4th −3 days	−0.713	−1.17	0.243	0.58
July 4th −2 days	0.245	0.40	0.188	0.45
July 4th −1 day	−1.157	−1.90	0.553	1.32
July 4th	−0.326	−0.54	0.038	0.09
July 4th +1 day	0.549	0.90	−0.139	−0.33
July 4th +2 days	0.193	0.32	−0.186	−0.45
July 4th +3 days	0.153	0.25	0.692	1.65
July 4th +4 days	−0.604	−0.99	−0.370	−0.88
Christmas −4 days	0.364	0.60	−0.327	−0.78
Christmas −3 days	−0.213	−0.35	−0.493	−1.17
Christmas −2 days	−1.579	−2.59*	−0.498	−1.18
Christmas −1 day	−1.228	−2.01*	−0.440	−1.05
Christmas day	−0.573	−0.94	−0.575	−1.37
Christmas +1 day	−0.471	−0.77	0.188	0.45
Christmas +2 days	−0.538	−0.88	−0.436	−1.04
Christmas +3 days	−0.558	−0.91	0.184	0.44

TABLE 10-1. (*Continued*)

Predictor variables	Males		Females	
	Coefficient	t	Coefficient	t
Labor Day −4 days	−0.287	−0.47	−0.160	−0.38
Labor Day −3 days	0.713	1.17	−0.075	−0.18
Labor Day −2 days	−0.802	−1.32	0.271	0.65
Labor Day −1 day	0.340	0.56	−0.863	−2.06*
Labor Day	0.351	0.57	0.097	0.23
Labor Day +1 day	1.441	2.35*	0.477	1.13
Labor Day +2 days	0.370	0.60	0.886	2.10*
Labor Day +3 days	1.031	1.68	−0.056	−0.13
Labor Day +4 days	0.743	1.21	0.854	2.02*
Memorial Day −4 days	−0.377	−0.61	−0.035	−0.08
Memorial Day −3 days	−0.495	−0.81	0.150	0.36
Memorial Day −2 days	−0.573	−0.93	0.371	0.88
Memorial Day −1 day	−0.447	−0.73	0.668	1.58
Memorial Day	−2.111	−3.44*	−1.000	−2.37*
Memorial Day +1 day	0.024	0.04	0.429	1.02
Memorial Day +2 days	−0.007	−0.01	−0.025	−0.06
Memorial Day +3 days	−0.250	−0.41	−0.270	−0.65
Memorial Day +4 days	−0.052	−0.09	−0.874	−2.09*
Thanksgiving −4 days	0.213	0.35	0.003	0.01
Thanksgiving −3 days	−0.632	−1.03	−0.259	−0.62
Thanksgiving −2 days	−0.648	−1.06	−0.684	−1.62
Thanksgiving −1 day	−0.929	−1.52	−0.896	−2.13*
Thanksgiving day	−0.919	−1.50	−0.550	−1.31
Thanksgiving +1 day	−0.133	−0.22	−0.145	−0.35
Thanksgiving +2 days	−0.436	−0.71	0.283	0.67
Thanksgiving +3 days	0.349	0.57	0.234	0.56
Thanksgiving +4 days	0.273	0.45	0.208	0.50
Year: 1968	−1.205	−6.41*	1.383	10.64*
Year: 1969	−1.021	−5.44*	1.441	11.09*
Year: 1970	−0.731	−3.89*	1.753	13.41*
Year: 1971	−0.864	−4.61*	1.967	15.00*
Year: 1972	−0.417	−2.23*	1.804	13.80*
Year: 1973	−0.687	−3.67*	1.231	9.50*
Year: 1974	−0.606	−3.23*	1.355	10.43*
Year: 1975	−0.494	−2.64*	1.076	8.32*
Year: 1976	−0.675	−3.60*	1.057	8.17*
Year: 1977	−0.291	−1.55	1.082	8.36*
Year: 1978	−0.425	−2.27*	0.481	3.73*
Year: 1979	−0.742	−3.96*	0.535	4.15*
Year: 1980	−0.874	−4.66*	0.170	1.32
Year: 1981	−0.641	−3.42*	0.336	2.61*
Year: 1982	−0.332	−1.77	0.403	3.12*
Year: 1983	−0.231	−1.23	0.106	0.83
Year: 1984	−0.238	−1.27	0.142	1.11

* Indicates a regression coefficient statistically significant at .05 or better, two-tailed t test.

(implicit) comparison year of 1985. The figures suggest that California male suicide levels were very gradually rising over the period 1968–1985. In contrast, female suicide levels in California seemed to be slowly declining during this time period. Both trends were weak; their explanation is presently unknown.

In examining Table 10-2, we turn to the central questions of this chapter: Does the Werther effect pervade all segments of society? Is it concentrated in some groups and not in others? Column 1 of Table 10-2 displays the total rise in suicides (correcting for the effect of other variables) in the observation period after the suicide story. It is evident that nearly all demographic groups displayed a rise in suicides after publicized suicide stories. Only persons aged 30–39 displayed a statistically insignificant drop in suicides after these stories. However, although the Werther effect was pervasive, it was quite small for nearly all groups, with the notable exception of teenagers. For this group, the daily rise in suicides during the observation period was approximately 22%. (This figure was calculated in the following fashion: Column 1 gives the total increase in suicides above normal during the 8-day observation period following the suicide story; the *daily* increase in suicides was one-eighth of this figure. When this daily increase was divided by the normal daily number of suicides [Column 2], we obtained an estimate of the size of the story effect.) It is interesting to note that teenagers behaved very differently from the next highest age group; this suggests that future studies of "youth" suicide should not lump together teens and young adults, as has frequently been the case to date.

One might expect the Werther effect to be stronger for groups that are already strongly predisposed to suicide. By this logic, a suicide story is most likely to trigger suicides in those who are already "close to the edge." However, the findings shown in Table 10-2 do not seem to support this expectation:

1. The male suicide rate was much higher than the female rate, but the Werther effect seemed to be no stronger for males than for females.
2. The white suicide rate was higher than that for blacks, but the Werther effect was not bigger for whites than for blacks.
3. The nonmarried suicide rate was higher than the rate for married people, but the Werther effect was not larger for unmarried people.
4. Those of retirement age typically have the highest suicide rates of all age groups, but the Werther effect for those who were retired seemed to be small, not large.

TABLE 10-2. Size of Story Effect for Various Demographic Groups, California, 1968–1985

Demographic group	Total rise in suicides 0–7 days after the suicide story	Average no. of daily suicides during the year	t	Rank of story effect vs. effect of other variables	Percentage increase per day 0–7 days after the suicide story
Male	3.048	6.25	2.66	2	6.09
Female	1.593	2.92	2.02	5	6.82
Teenagers	0.985	0.56	2.87	1	22.08
Age 20–29	1.159	2.07	1.74	2	6.99
Age 30–39	−0.059	1.57	−0.10	56	−0.47
Age 40–49	0.774	1.41	1.46	3	6.87
Age 50–64	1.267	1.98	1.98	2	8.01
Retired	0.547	1.59	0.94	9	4.30
Married	2.258	3.79	2.54	4	7.44
Nonmarried	3.043	4.87	3.05	4	7.82
White	3.985	8.52	2.99	2	5.84
Nonwhite	0.660	0.65	1.79	3	12.73
Suicide at home[a]	4.103	8.46	3.09	2	6.06
Suicide not at home	0.532	0.71	1.37	2	9.32

[a]The term "suicide at home" signifies a death for which the county of residence was the same as the county of death. The term "suicide not at home" signifies a death for which the county of death was not the county of residence.

Only persons dying away from home provided some tentative support for the notion that unintegrated people are most prone to imitative suicide: The Werther effect was slightly stronger for persons dying outside their county of residence than it was for persons dying at home. However, this evidence must be considered to have ambiguous implications, since it is by no means certain that persons who kill themselves away from home are on the average less socially integrated than persons who kill themselves at home.

Thus far, we have been discussing the size of the story effect in terms of a percentage increase above the normal level of suicides. It is interesting to consider the size of the story effect in a different fashion, by comparing the the story effect with the effects of other variables known to influence suicide. Column 4 of Table 10-2 summarizes a great many comparisons of this sort. For example, the figure "1" in this column associated with teenagers indicates that the effect of a suicide story in the 8-day observation period was larger than the effect of any of the other 88 variables analyzed in the regression equation: day of the week, month, holidays, and so on. Similarly, the figure "2" for persons aged 20–29 indicates that for this group the suicide story had the second largest effect of all the variables considered.[4]

Discussion

It is evident from Table 10-2 that for nearly all demographic groups, suicide stories have an unusually large effect, in comparison with the effect of other temporal variables. This conclusion needs to be qualified in various ways. First, although the effect of the average suicide story is far greater than the effect of (say) the average Wednesday, the cumulative effect of Wednesdays is far greater than the cumulative effect of suicide stories, because there are so many more Wednesdays than suicide stories. Second, although the effect of a suicide story is large when compared with the effect of temporal variables (e.g., day of the week, month, etc.), it is not large when compared with the effect of demographic variables (e.g., age, race, and sex). Thus, it may be wisest to consider that for most segments of society, the suicide story exerts an effect that is not so small as to be negligible nor so large as to preclude consideration of all other etiological factors.

A somewhat different conclusion seems appropriate for teenagers, for whom the suicide story does seem to exert a very important effect.

---

[4] One may wish to recast this analysis by comparing the story effect with the total effect of each holiday: HOL (−4) + HOL (−3), . . . , + HOL (+4). Even when this is done, however, the effect of the story remains pre-eminent.

Teenagers

For this group, it seems appropriate to consider ways of reducing the harmful effect of suicide stories.

It is worth noting that, in comparison with all the other temporal and demographic variables under discussion, the suicide story seems most amenable to social control. One cannot plausibly abolish Mondays, even though they are associated with a significant rise in suicides. Nor can one transform whites into nonwhites so as to reduce their predisposition to suicide. But it is possible to reduce the publicity accorded to suicide stories and to change the manner in which the suicide story is reported.

One way to address this issue is to consider the suicide story as a type of "natural advertisement." Studies of advertising suggest that the effect of an advertisement is reduced if it is treated in the following way:

1. If the advertisement is not repeated. Thus, suicide stories (or advertisements) appearing on a single program seem to have a smaller effect than multiprogram stories or advertisements.

2. If the advertisement is placed in an obscure location. Cover-page advertisements in magazines are more expensive because they are thought to be more effective. Similarly, Phillips (unpublished research) *Newspaper* found that front-page suicide stories had a detectable effect, whereas inside-page stories did not. This suggests that some suicide stories might be moved to inside sections of the newspapers.

3. If the characters in the advertisement are presented in a neutral or unsympathetic light. People are probably less likely to imitate a character in an advertisement (or suicide story) if it is difficult to identify with him or her.

4. If the negative consequences of the advertised behavior are mentioned in the advertisement. Thus, the inclusion of the Surgeon General's warning is designed to reduce the impact of cigarette commercials. It is noteworthy that suicide stories typically fail to mention negative consequences (e.g., pain and disfigurement) that often accompany a suicide. It is possible that if these things were mentioned in a realistic description of the suicide story, this would reduce the level of imitation.

5. If the advertisement mentions alternatives to the advertised product. Commercial advertisements never mention competing products (unless with the intent of disparaging them). Thus a McDonald's commercial does not mention Burger King or Kentucky Fried Chicken. It is interesting to note that the "natural advertisement" of a suicide story often has the same monolithic character: The story focuses on one response to psychological anguish—suicide—without indicating that there are many other possible responses as well. It is possible that mention of these alternatives (hotlines, counseling, self-help groups, etc.) in the suicide story would reduce the tendency to imitative suicide.

Nearly 150 years ago, the British Registrar General of Births, Deaths, and Marriages asked rather plaintively in his annual report, "Why should cases of suicide be recorded at length in public papers any more than cases of fever?" (General Register Office of Great Britain, 1841). The imitative behavior that prompted this question still exists today, and we need to remain concerned about the impact of publicized suicide stories. Our solution to the problem need not be Draconian, however. It seems likely that the effects of these stories can be greatly reduced by changing the manner in which they are reported, rather than by omitting them entirely from the news.

TECHNICAL APPENDIX

1. Test for autocorrelation. The conventional test for autocorrelation (employing the Durbin–Watson statistic) is inappropriate when a lagged dependent variable is used, as in the present analysis (Durbin, 1970; Johnston, 1972). Instead, Durbin's second test (Durbin, 1970) was used. After correcting for the effects of the other independent variables used in the regression analysis, we found no relationship between the residual on day t and the residual on day $t + 1$ (for males, the coefficient was 0.2573, $t = 0.71$; for females, equivalent figures were -0.3394 and -1.09). Hence, there was no evidence of first-order autocorrelation of the residuals. Autocorrelation of higher orders was sought by calculating the autocorrelation and partial autocorrelation functions for orders 1 through 30. All correlations were very small (ranging between -0.044 and $+0.044$) and displayed no evident pattern.

2. Test for heteroscedasticity. Glejser's test (Glejser, 1969) revealed evidence of mild but statistically significant heteroscedasticity for males and for females. However, when the dependent variable was subjected to the commonly used Freeman–Tukey transformation (Freeman & Tukey, 1950) (as recommended by Weisberg, 1980), evidence of heteroscedasticity disappeared: After the transformation, the independent variables in the regression equation were uncorrelated with the absolute value of the residual. For males, $R^2 = 1.7\%$; adjusted $R^2 = 0.3\%$; F (88, 6,485) = 1.253, $p > .05$. For females, $R^2 = 1.6\%$; adjusted $R^2 = 0.2\%$; F (88, 6,485) = 1.185; $p > .05$. After the Freeman–Tukey transformation, the effect of suicide stories remained significant for males ($t = 2.64$) and for females ($t = 2.13$).

Following Weisberg (1980), we plotted residuals from the regression equations and found no evidence linking the size of the residual to the expected number of suicides per day. A normal probability plot of the standardized residuals indicated that the distribution of standardized residuals fit the normal very closely.

The analyses above indicate that the effect of the suicide story cannot be plausibly ascribed to heteroscedasticity or to autocorrelation.

References

Bollen, K. A., & Phillips, D. P. Suicidal motor vehicle fatalities in Detroit: A replication. *American Journal of Sociology*, 1981, *87*, 404–412.

Bollen, K. A., & Phillips, D. P. Imitative suicides: A national study of the effects of television news stories. *American Sociological Review*, 1982, *47*, 802–809.

Crawford, J. P., & Willis, J. H. Double suicide in psychiatric hospital patients. *British Journal of Psychiatry*, 1966, *112*, 1231–1235.

Durkheim, E. *Suicide*. Glencoe, Ill.: Free Press, 1951. (Originally published, 1897.)

Durbin, J. Testing for serial correlation in least-squares regression when some of the regressors are lagged dependent variables. *Econometrica*, 1970, *38*, 410–421.

Freeman, M. F., & Tukey, J. W. Transformations related to the angular and the square root. *Annals of Mathematical Statistics*, 1950, *21*, 607–611.

General Register Office of Great Britain. *The Registrar General's annual report on births, deaths, and marriages, 1841*. London: Her Majesty's Stationery Office, 1841.

Glejser, H. A new test for heteroscedasticity. *Journal of the American Statistical Association*, 1969, *64*, 316–23.

Gould, M. S., & Shaffer, D. The impact of suicide in television movies: Evidence of imitation. *New England Journal of Medicine*, 1986, *315*, 690–694.

Gray, R. *Goethe: A critical introduction*. Cambridge, England: Cambridge University Press, 1967.

Johnston, J. *Econometric methods* (2nd ed.). New York: McGraw-Hill, 1972.

Kreitman, N., Smith, P., & Tan, E. Attempted suicide in social networks. *British Journal of Preventive and Social Medicine*, 1969, *23*, 116–123.

Motto, J. A. Suicide and suggestibility. *American Journal of Psychiatry*, 1967, *124*, 252–256.

Pell, B., & Watters, D. Newspaper policies on suicide stories. *Canada's Mental Health*, 1982, *30*, 8–9.

Phelps, E. Neurotic books and newspapers as factors in the mortality of suicide and crime. *Journal of Social Medicine*, 1911, *12*, 264–306.

Phillips, D. P. The influence of suggestion on suicide: Substantive and theoretical implications of the Werther effect. *American Sociological Review*, 1974, *39*, 340–354.

Phillips, D. P. Motor vehicle fatalities increase just after publicized suicide stories. *Science*, 1977, *196*, 1464–1465.

Phillips, D. P. Suicide, motor vehicle fatalities, and the mass media: Evidence toward a theory of suggestion. *American Journal of Sociology*, 1979, *84*, 1150–1174.

Phillips, D. P., & Carstensen, L. L. Clustering of teenage suicides after television news stories about suicide. *New England Journal of Medicine*, 1986, *315*, 685–689.

Phillips, D. P., & Paight, D. J. The impact of televised movies about suicide: A replicative study. *New England Journal of Medicine*, 1987, *317*, 809–811.

Phillips, D. P., Paight, D. J., & Carstensen, L. L. Effects of mass media stories on suicides, with new evidence on the role of story content. In C. Pfeffer (Ed.), *New biopsychosocial perspectives on youth suicide*. NY: American Psychiatric Press, in press.

Phillips, D. P., & Sanzone, A. A comparison of injury date and death date in 42,698 suicides. *American Journal of Public Health*, May, 1988.

Phillips, D. P., & Wills, J. S. A drop in suicides around major national holidays. *Suicide and Life-Threatening Behavior*, 1987, *17*, 1–12.

Platt, S. The aftermath of Angie's overdose: Is soap (opera) dangerous to your health? *British Medical Journal*, 1987, *294*, 954–957.

Rose, W. Introduction. In J. W. von Goethe, *The sorrows of young Werther*. London: Scholastic Press, 1929.

Schmidtke, A., & Hafner, H. Die vermittlung von selbstmordmotivation und selbst-
mordhandlung durch fiktive modelle. Nervenarzt, 1986, 57, 502–510.
Seiden, R. H. Suicide behavior contagion on a college campus. In N. L. Farberow (Ed.),
Proceedings of the Fourth International Conference on Suicide Prevention. Los Angeles:
Delmaro, 1968.
Stack, S. The effect of suggestion on suicide: A reassessment. Paper presented at the
annual meeting of the American Sociological Association, San Antonio, Texas, August
1984.
Stack, S. Celebrities and suicides: A taxonomy and analysis. American Sociological
Review, 1987, 52, 401–412.
Wasserman, I. Imitation and suicide: A reexamination of the Werther effect. American
Sociological Review, 1984, 49, 427–436.
Weisberg, S. Applied linear regression. New York: Wiley, 1980.
Weiss, E. The clinical significance of the anniversary reaction. General Practitioner,
1958, 17, 117–119.

Index